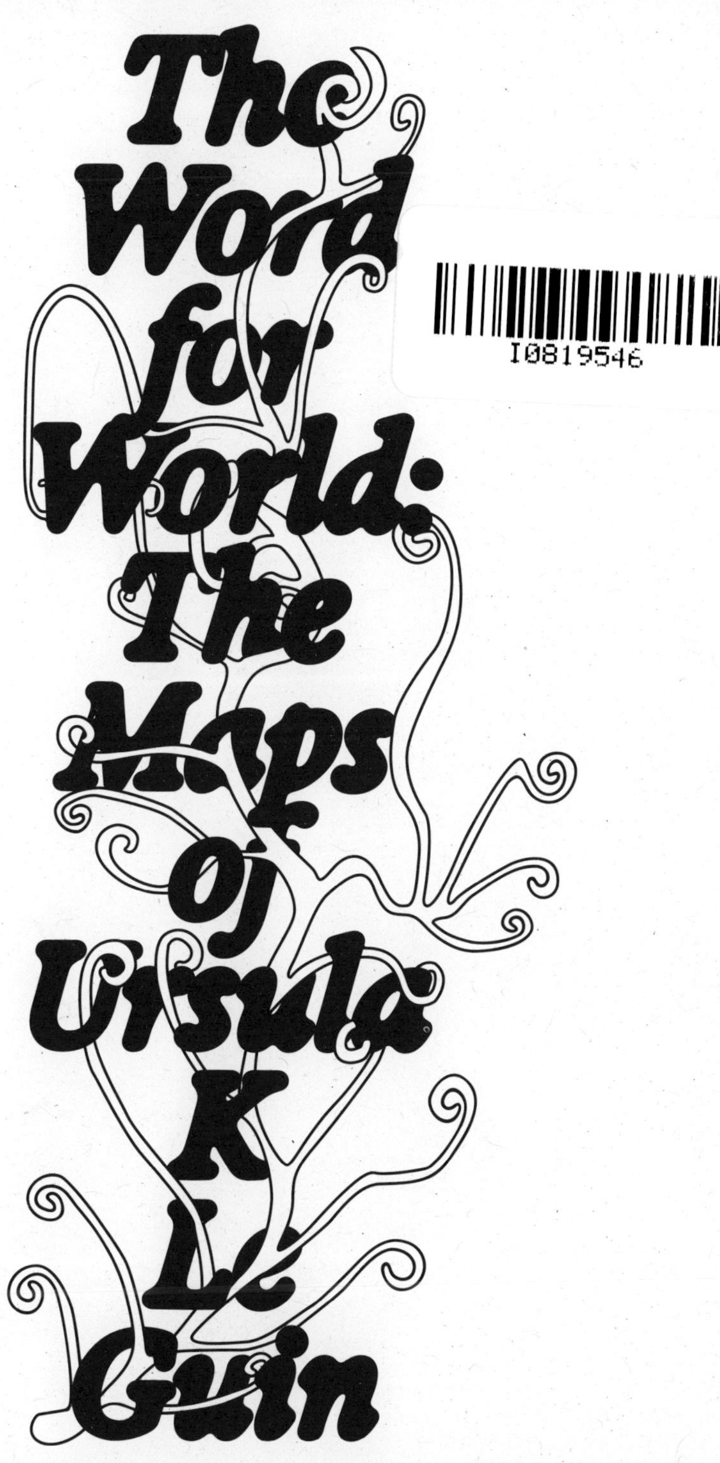
The Word for World: The Maps of Ursula K Le Guin

The Word for World: The Maps of Ursula K Le Guin

Edited by So Mayer and Sarah Shin

First published in 2025 by Silver Press
and AA Publications

The dragon should not be snaky/bat-like –
It is a beautiful fiery creature.

A bit of spiky tail
could be visible
thro' mists

The wings should
be scaled or jewelled –
not bat-like

The dragon must
have triangular
points along its back –
this is mentioned often
in the books. Its eyes
are large + intelligent-looking – and
It has LEGS – with big dragony CLAWS!

There should be an indication
of scales, with a metallic
gleam to them – not smooth
skin – on the body + arms

Ursula K Le Guin's instructions on how to draw a dragon,
directed to the cover artist for *The Other Wind* (2001).

So Mayer and Sarah Shin

Introduction

Pandora Can't Read the Map

The Word for World is Forest

In Ursula K Le Guin's 1972 novella *The Word for World is Forest*, Athshe is a planet comprised of ocean and forest. Its indigenous people, the Athsheans, are small in stature, covered in green fur and have a polycyclic sleep pattern. A peaceful, matriarchal society, the Athsheans practice competitive singing instead of physical fighting, a ritual act which contains conflict and dispels antagonistic energy within a social system of ceremony. Their word for 'world' is the same as their word for 'forest'.

The Athsheans are a dreaming culture, living and dreaming in worldly and mythical time – two imbricated, simultaneous realities whose connection is profound but obscure. Their aptitude in dreaming awake corresponds to their affinity with the trees of the forest in which they dwell, and which resides within them. The substance of the Athshean world is forest; their entangled roots are a collective dream. Adept dreamers are lucid in the non-local dream-time, 'the springs of reality', as well as the localised world-time, 'the dead world of action'. They move into the dream reality to speak with ancestors, divine answers and draw sustenance – for 'Once you have learned to do your dreaming wide awake, to balance your sanity not on the razor's edge of reason but on the double support, the fine balance, of reason and dream; once you have learned that, you cannot unlearn it any more than you can unlearn to think.'[1]

Their colonisers, Terran humans, consider the Athsheans subhuman for their queer dreamy passivity and exploit them as slave labour on their New Tahiti logging colony. The destruction of the forest is the destruction of the Athsheans, for whom spiritual and social life, habitat, sovereignty and language inform one another. As one island after another is shattered by deforestation, the Athshean protagonist Selver leads an attack on the Terran camp: to awaken from the 'evil dream' of Terran occupation, they steal and take into their own hands the fire they feared – but Selver only harms the Terran camp leader Captain Davidson in dream, singing over him in world-time. Under 'the green-gold shadows of the ash leaves', Selver reflects on their exchange.

> 'Sometimes a god comes,' Selver said. 'He brings a new way to do a thing, or a new thing to be done. A new kind of singing, or a new kind of death. He brings this across the bridge between the dream-time and the world-time. When he has done this, it is done. You cannot take things that exist in the world and try to drive them back into the dream, to hold them inside the dream with walls and pretenses. That is insanity. What is, is. There is no use pretending, now, that we do not know how to kill one another.'[2]

This book and accompanying exhibition at the Architectural Association (AA) both borrow their title, *The Word for World*, from Le Guin's novella. They begin from where her fable ends: in a world in which a new kind of singing and a new kind of death have already come into being. Through centuries of epistemic violence and colonial capitalism, ours is a time so separated from the dream that we remain asleep in the nightmare of reason. If the Athshean word for world is forest, what other words could ours be?

When Le Guin started writing a new story, she would begin by drawing a map. This book and the exhibition present a selection of these maps and responses to them to ask: how do her imaginary worlds enable us to re-envision our own? From a young age, Le Guin's imagination was seeded by the books she read in the library of her father, Alfred Kroeber, an influential anthropologist – ranging from mythologies from around the world, to Lao Tzu's *Tao Te Ching*, to French classics and British modernists – while Napa Valley, where the Le Guin family spent their summers, inspired the ur-place, where space becomes time, in *Always Coming Home* (1985). The influence of her early encounters with such a variety of stories and philosophies of time and space can be seen across her work, in which she explores, for instance, how to travel across the galaxy. Expanding modern, Westernised ideas about representation and reality, in Le Guin's worlds, a dream or a story, too, can be a map.

The Word for World exhibition's dream-like design by Standard Deviation draws from Le Guin's holistic approach to narrative and place, especially the fractal notion from *The Dispossessed* (1974) that 'to be part is to be whole'. Each map is a world in itself, and a part of the world: the exhibition interprets the landforms and structures shown by the maps – forest, valley, archipelago, mountain, and house – to create an otherworldly place in itself.

Similarly, this book brings together contributions from a variety of perspectives and practices to respond to Le Guin's maps, weaving together many words for worlds. Many kinds of writing – including personal essays, stories, interviews, poems and recipes – meditate on the shared ability of maps and language to recall what has been and to call into being. Shoshone Collective enter their ancestral forest to map traditional foodways, reconnecting land with its peoples, its songs and senses; while Bhanu Kapil takes her reader into a forest of bewilderment in her prose poem 'The Clearing': 'The forest moves in an anti-clockwise fashion, then clockwise again.'

Theo Downes-Le Guin reflects on the places, images and experiences from which his mother drew her maps, including the places in California and Oregon that knew her best, and David Naimon connects this to Le Guin's poetry of place, and to what water can teach.

For poets Canisia Lubrin and Nisha Ramayya, the riverine maps of the Valley of the Kesh, from *Always Coming Home*, open up ways to name and live in the connected complexities of the present. Likewise, anthropologist Marilyn Strathern and philosopher Federico Campagna range across the interconnected postcolonial networks of our living planet, thinking about migration and/as being in place. Una McCormack and Daniel Heath

Justice, science fiction and fantasy authors respectively, follow the curves of maps in genre fiction as offerings to writers and thinkers, with McCormack tracing the map of the labyrinth from *The Tombs of Atuan* (1970) as a way-finder for her life, and Heath Justice reflecting on maps as a place where fantasy novels and Cherokee scholarship overlay each other.

At the centre, like the Athshean ash tree, or Roke, the heart of Earthsea, is Standard Deviation's 'Legend', an index of story – weaving together an invented cosmogonic myth with dreams and inspirations from the lives of Le Guin and the exhibition makers – with a map and an experimental non-Euclidean architectural plan of the exhibition room at the AA.

Earthsea

The map for *A Wizard of Earthsea* (1968) is as much a poem as it is a diagram, a saga-like rolling recitation of names giving the sense that the careful, fractal sketches of coastlines are not just realisations of descriptions in the novel (the Hands really are shaped like hands), but a mnemonic: a carrier bag for a fiction made up of artfully drawn lines, to which names are attached like charms on a charm bracelet.

It is not the earliest of Le Guin's maps: those are the diagrams and charts of the seasons and years on Werel from *Planet of Exile* (1966), a set of guidemaps to help the author in planning a novel set on a planet with an orbital period of 60 Earth years, and correspondingly complex seasonal shifts. Her earliest maps for a fantasy novel, the Orsinian maps for the historical romance *Malafrena* (published in 1979, but written much earlier), are fairly traditional European overviews and insets, made for a novel that borrows from Romantic realism for its revolutionary alternate history. It is an imaginative leap from the coach-and-horse routes through Orsinia to the expansive Archipelago of *A Wizard of Earthsea*, moving from a human scale to a dragon's-eye view of the islands spilling out across the sea.

In her 2012 afterword to *A Wizard of Earthsea*, Le Guin writes:

> But *where* is as important in the realms of pure imagination as it is here in mundanity. Before I started to write the story, I got a big piece of poster-board and drew the map. I drew all the islands of Earthsea, the Archipelago, the Kargad Lands, and the Reaches. And I named them: Havnor, the great island in the middle of the world; Selidor, far out in the west, and the Dragon's Run, and Hur-at-Hur, and all the rest. But only as I sailed with Ged from Gont did I begin to know the islands, one by one. With him, I first came to Roke, and the Ninety Isles, and Osskil, and farther east even than Astowell.[3]

Le Guin learned to sail off the coast of California, and her book on creative writing *Steering the Craft* (1998) uses sailing as a metaphor for writing and editing. When she first set her mind to devising a high fantasy world, it is a sea world. As a large-scale sailing chart, such as might be kept by the Master Windkey, one of the wizards with whom Ged studies on Roke, *A Wizard of Earthsea*'s map is expressive of its protagonist's adventure; like Le Guin, we sail with Ged from Gont to Roke at the centre, and then centrifugally to all four corners, and even off the map.

In the second book in the series, Ged reaches the hostile Kargad Lands in the north-east, but *The Tombs of Atuan* is not told from his perspective. The maps for that book are not those of a traveller: rather they are scaled to the knowledge held by Tenar, the priestess of the Undertomb, as Una McCormack discusses in this volume. There is an overground map constrained to the grounds of the temple where Tenar has lived since she was a child; and there is an underground map of the labyrinth, of which only she and a few others have knowledge. What might appear as a promise of material treasure instead leads the way to freedom.

Robert Louis Stevenson popularised treasure maps in adventure fiction through the enormous success of *Treasure Island* (1883), drawing the reader into the action with a map of a world entirely predicated on colonisation, conquest and exploitation. Such a world is defined by what Le Guin calls 'the wonderful, poisonous story ... The killer story'.[4] Le Guin's short story 'Sur', a gentle parody of the age of heroic adventuring, reverses this: her adventurers to the South Pole are all Latin American women (one of them pregnant), travelling a decade before Roald Amundsen and keeping their achievement to themselves so as not to upset the men. The story begins with one adventurer's descendant finding the map that the women drew.

Sometimes a map comes to you. In the US edition of Le Guin's short story collection *The Compass Rose* (1982), the map appears as the second page of the story, with the subtitle 'The Map in the Attic', although her original sketch has both its place names and its title in Spanish, 'El Mapa en el desván'.[5] Alongside recognisable names that European explorers gave to features of Antarctica, there's Florence Nightingale Glacier and Mt Bolívar's Big Nose: the feminist rewriting of a successful expedition to the South Pole is why we included the story in Silver Press' collection of Le Guin's writings on feminism and anarchism, *Space Crone* (2023).

'Sur' appears as the final story in *The Compass Rose*: the collection is organised geographically into six sections, with North at the top/start, and South at the bottom/end, including Nadir and Zenith alongside the traditional compass points. Le Guin draws her commitment to the six directions from 'many of the American peoples who were dispossessed by the compass-guided invaders from the East'. In her preface, she writes:

> The stories... take place all over the map, including the margins. It is not even clear to me what the map is a map of. A mind, no doubt; presumably the

> author's. But I expect there is more to it than that. One's mind is never simply one's own, even at birth, and ever less so as one lives, learns, loses, etc... As a guide to sailors, this book is not to be trusted. Perhaps it is too sensitive to local magnetic fields.[6]

Le Guin encourages readers and writers to remain sensitive to local magnetic fields, to spin like the needle of the compass as we navigate the relation between world and story. Her reconfigured map of Antarctica is a reminder that maps are human artefacts; they are contingent fictions at which we, too, can try our hands.

The Dispossessed

Maps may be drawn by the author, but they are the opposite of authoritative. In the foreword to the collection *The Birthday of the World and Other Stories* (2002), Le Guin remarks of her Hainish cosmos:

> Though I've put a good deal of work into my fictional universe, I don't exactly feel that I invented it. I blundered into it, and have been blundering around in it unsystematically ever since – dropping a millennium here, forgetting a planet there...
>
> I did not plan these worlds and people. I found them, gradually, piecemeal, while writing stories. I'm still finding them.[7]

Le Guin found her fictional worlds through mapping. She brings a striking graphic clarity and simplicity to the hemispheric maps of Gethen, the world of 'Winter's King' and *The Left Hand of Darkness* (both 1969), and of Urras and Anarres, for *The Dispossessed*, which speak to Le Guin's grounding in Taoist non-duality: balancing, not mirroring. 'Light is the left hand of darkness / and darkness the right hand of light', goes the Gethenian song 'Tormer's Lay' that gives *The Left Hand of Darkness* its title, a principle expressed in Le Guin's maps of their world.[8]

The Dispossessed is a tale of two worlds. Detailed hemispheric maps appear at the start of the novel, first of Anarres, the anarchist moon where the protagonist Shevek grows up, and then of Urras, the 'parent' planet to which he travels. Each chapter then features stylised iconic renderings of two hemispheres. Shevek's schoolfriend Tirin comments one evening as they are sitting on a hill under the stars,

> I never thought before... of the fact that there are people sitting on a hill, up there, on Urras, looking at Anarres, at us, and saying 'Look, there's the Moon.' Our earth is their Moon; our Moon is their earth.[9]

Shevek will be the only member of his generation to look at each planet as a moon; he will return to Anarres, seeing it differently. The hemispheric maps that look across at each other, as it were, express the novel's foundational philosophy that 'true journey is return'.

The Western Shore

Theo Downes-Le Guin's contribution to this volume speaks in more detail about his mother's sense of place in Oregon and California, expressed most strongly in the one mode of her writing that does not include maps, perhaps because it is its own form of mnemonic: her poetry. As David Naimon discusses in his contribution, Le Guin's poems in *Out Here* (2010), in particular, are oracular maps. As far back as 1988, in the collection *Wild Oats & Fireweed*, Le Guin was hoeing her rows in lines of poetry, knowing her place through words.

Her poems share this affinity for the local with her late novels: the standalone historical novel *Lavinia* (2008) and *Voices* (2006), which is part of the Annals of the Western Shore fantasy trilogy. Both novels feature young protagonists facing occupying armies, equipped only with their deep local knowledge, expressed in the detailed maps that accompany their stories. For *Lavinia*,

Le Guin steeped herself in the words of Virgil's epic poem *The Aeneid*, but unlike 'Sur', Le Guin does not insert a witty feminist critique into the map. Instead, the map returns to the local scale and European conventions of the Orsinian maps, but also shows the influence of *Searoad* (1991) and *Always Coming Home*, with their close relations to known places on this Earth. The map labelled 'Latium meum' draws on the archaeological record of pre-Roman Etruscans to give us Lavinia's understanding of her land before the arrival of the Trojans.

The archaeological precision of the map contrasts with Lavinia, who knows herself to be a character created by Virgil for *The Aeneid*; but she is able to call him to her, and debate with him, through a deep attunement to her beloved place. Memer in *Voices* dwells with the same attunement, despite having lived under a totalitarian occupation since birth. Quick-witted Memer is taught to read and write by her guardian, a big risk under the anti-literate, misogynist, monotheistic occupiers; dressed in boy's clothes as a groom, Memer becomes Mem in order to traverse the city of Ansul. Gathering groceries and information, Mem also maps the city through small observances to Ansul's many gods. Both spiritual and practical knowledge will help Mem/er save lives and challenge the occupation.

The map of Ansul at the start of *Voices* is a document of resistance in a city where writing, reading, and ritual observance are banned. Like the maps in *Always Coming Home*, it protects a beloved place talismanically. In *Voices*, certain books in Mem/er's house speak and even bleed; maps, too, might be alive.

Always Coming Home

> I was studying yet once more the contours of my map of the region, when it dawned as slowly and certainly as the sun itself upon me that the town was there, between the creeks, under my feet the whole time.[10]

In *Always Coming Home*, Pandora is looking for Sinshan, the town of the Kesh people, which Le Guin describes as 'going to have existed a long, long time from now'. She consults a map of the region, but cannot use it to locate the town in the valleys of what will no longer be northern California in the distant, post-apocalyptic future. Pandora can't read the map, but it turns out the map isn't necessary: her speculative archaeology of the future is a practice not of digging, but of attending to the landscape, seeing with the mind's eye and hearing with the inner ear.

Gathering the stories of the future-past Kesh, including the main narrator Stone Telling's autobiography, songs, recipes, rituals and other cultural artefacts, together with Pandora's present-day search, *Always Coming Home* is a multi-dimensional map – a myth – that invites the reader to unmake assumptions encoded by a two-dimensional one. Le Guin explains in her essay 'A Non-Euclidean View of California as a Cold Place to Be' that mythic space-time, or 'the Golden Age, or Dream Time, is remote only from the rational mind. It is not accessible to euclidean reason; but on the evidence of all myth and mysticism, and the assurance of every participatory religion, it is, to those with the gift or discipline to perceive it, right here, right now.'[11] Sinshan turns out to be underneath Pandora's feet, once she is able to perceive it by reading the landscape through a symbolic logic at the scale of the world. This is a scale of meaning created through relationships: between the centre and the periphery, the part and the whole and the world and its representation.

California was not a 'wilderness' or chaos before the settler cartography mapped it; it was known because 'Every hill, every valley, creek, canyon, gulch, gully, draw, point, cliff, bluff, beach, bend, good-sized boulder, and tree of any character had its name, its place in the order of things.'[12] Each named place was 'not a goal, not a place to get to, but a place where one is: a center of the world. There were centers of the world all over California.'[13] In the history of settler colonialism, 'one of our finest methods of organized forgetting is called discovery',[14] but where one is – one's centre or 'lived time, the place people call home, the seventh direction' – is within a present that remembers.[15]

A seeker may consult a conventional map to find something that they don't yet have, but in a world of many centres, maps are not tools for finding. The Kesh of *Always Coming Home*, the people of the Valley, draw maps of what they already know well: the Valley. In fact, 'the better they knew them, the better they liked to draw and map them'. Since they knew the landscape so well, maps 'were less guides than talismans'.[16] A talismanic map is not oriented towards the future; in fact, a person of the Valley 'doesn't perceive time as a direction, let alone a progress, but as a landscape in which one may go any number of directions, or nowhere'.[17]

A talismanic map is symbolic, powerful – locating where one is in the landscape of time, which is 'not an arrow, nor a river, but a house, the house he lives in. One may go from room to room, and come back; to go outside, all you have to do is open the door.'[18] The Kesh house is both domestic architecture, and a House: a basic division of society that is materialised as the heyima. Translations such as 'church, temple, shrine, lodge' are inadequate to convey the Kesh term 'formed of the elements *heya, heyiya* – the connotations of which include sacredness, hinge, connection, spiral, center, praise, and change – and *ma*, house'.[19]

The idea of heyiya, 'the visual form of an idea which pervaded the thought and culture of the Valley', is represented by the double spiral, the heyiya-if. In a Valley town shaped like the double spiral, 'everybody had two houses: the house you lived in, your dwelling place, in the Left Arm ... and in the Right Arm, your House, the heyimas'.[20] One met with one's community in the heyima – an underground building with a roof-pyramid above ground. The map of the town of Sinshan on p 56 shows these houses figured on the two arms of the double spiral, that one may inhabit or go anywhere in. The map is the image of spatialised time – a house that one lives in, that contains both the physical house of dwelling and the greater House.

Such different layers of form, signification and storytelling are a part of the world in *Always Coming Home*'s metafiction, rather than systems of meaning kept separate from each other. Likewise, rather than attempting a realist model, Kesh maps are 'remarkably accurate, considering that their function was mostly aesthetic or poetic; but then, accuracy was considered a fundamental element or quality of poetry.' They take elements of landscape as their signs:

> maps of the Valley were always drawn as charts of the Na and its confluence, and maps of areas within the Valley took the principal creek or creek-system as their axis. The source of the stream is at the top of the map. Compass directions may be noted, but the map is oriented to the flow of water, and 'down' is the bottom of the page.[21]

The Other Wind

Maps are integral to *Always Coming Home*, a compendious carrier bag of Kesh life; they appeared in the book from its first edition. Other maps included in this volume have varied publication histories, from entirely unpublished to publication in some editions but not others; captions on published maps indicate the first publication date of the novel or story, which is not necessarily that of the map. Relations between sketches and published maps vary. In the case of Le Guin's best-known map of the Earthsea archipelago, not only does this volume quote two slightly different versions of the story of its first sketch, but the first edition of *A Wizard of Earthsea* included a map by cover artist Ruth Robbins, while subsequent editions and volumes of the Earthsea series have featured subtly different maps. This volume does not aim to be definitive, any more than Le Guin did: it is a mapping of imagination.

Le Guin's maps offer journeys of consciousness beyond conventional cartography, from Pandora's education in Kesh culture to the Rorschach-like archipelago of Earthsea. Rather than remaining within known terrain, they open up paradigms of knowledge, exemplified by the map's edges and how a map is read, made and remade, together. The world is where we are, and, at the same time, as Pandora says, 'we have a long way yet to go and I can't go without you'.[22]

For Le Guin, the collective unconscious and dreams share with mythology archetypal figures and the language of symbolism. In her 1976 essay 'Myth and Archetype in Science Fiction', she surmises, 'we all have the same kind of dragons in our psyche, just as we all have the same kind of heart and lungs in our body'. Myth releases such 'dragons, heroes, quests; objects of power, voyages at night and under sea' from the unconscious.[23]

In her essay 'Why are Americans Afraid of Dragons?' (1974), Le Guin identifies that an anti-dragon culture is anti-imagination. Such a culture continues to wreak havoc today by refusing to recognise and withdraw its shadow, which, Le Guin writes in 'The Child and the Shadow' (1975), stands 'on the threshold between the conscious and the unconscious mind, and we meet it in our dreams, as sister, brother, friend, beast, monster, enemy, guide. It is all we don't want to, can't admit into our conscious self, all the qualities and tendencies within us which have been repressed, denied, or not used.'[24]

Julie Phillips, currently writing the first authorised biography of Le Guin, shared with us a dragon that Le Guin had drawn as an instructional model for the cover illustration for the last Earthsea book, *The Other Wind* (2001). Therein, dragons and humans remember their shared ancestry, and its connection to the islands of the archipelago. The young King of the Archipelago, Lebannen, a friend of Ged's and Tenar's, is charged with bringing together a peace-making coalition to go and parlay with the dragons. On the journey, he remembers an old song that evokes the world before the map and the magic of the open spaces of the imagination into which change can flow:

O my joy!
Before bright Éa was, before Segoy
Bade the islands be,
The morning wind blew on the sea.
O my joy, be free! [25]

Hinting at the correspondence of the land and the dragon, Le Guin's dragon-map serves as a carrier of myth – collective memory and a guide to our future. We should remember her map well, as a talisman, for we have a long way yet to go. We will need the imagination she advocates for in her essay 'The Question I Get Asked Most Often' (2000/2003), where she warns, 'People who deny the existence of dragons are often eaten by dragons. From within.'[26]

So Mayer and Sarah Shin
June 2025
London, UK

1 Ursula K Le Guin, *The Word for World is Forest* (Tor, 2010), p 116.
2 Ibid, pp 188–9.
3 Le Guin, *The Books of Earthsea: The Complete Illustrated Edition* (Gollancz, 2018), pp 217–8.
4 Le Guin, *The Carrier Bag Theory of Fiction*, (Ignota, 2019), p 33.
5 Le Guin, *The Compass Rose* (Harper & Row, 1982), p 256.
6 Ibid, p vii.
7 Le Guin, *The Birthday of the World and Other Stories* (Gollancz, 2003), p viii.
8 Le Guin, *The Left Hand of Darkness* (Gollancz, 2017), p 233.
9 Le Guin, *The Dispossessed* (Harper & Row, 1974), p 36.
10 Le Guin, *Always Coming Home* (Grafton, 1988), p 3.
11 Le Guin, 'A Non-Euclidean View of California as a Cold Place to Be', in *Dreams Must Explain Themselves: The Selected Non-Fiction of Ursula K. Le Guin* (Gollancz, 2018), p 106.
12 Ibid, p 107.
13 Ibid.
14 Ibid, p 108.
15 Ibid, p 107.
16 Le Guin, *Always Coming Home,* p 450.
17 Ibid, p 171.
18 Ibid, p 171–2.
19 Ibid, p 45.
20 Ibid, pp 44–8.
21 Ibid, p 450.
22 Ibid, p 339.
23 Le Guin, 'Myth and Archetype in Science Fiction', in *The Language of the Night* (Women's Press, 1989), p 67.
24 Le Guin, 'The Child and the Shadow', in *The Language of the Night*, p 53.
25 Le Guin, *The Books of Earthsea*, p 861.
26 Le Guin, 'The Question I Get Asked Most Often', in *Dreams Must Explain Themselves*, p 269.

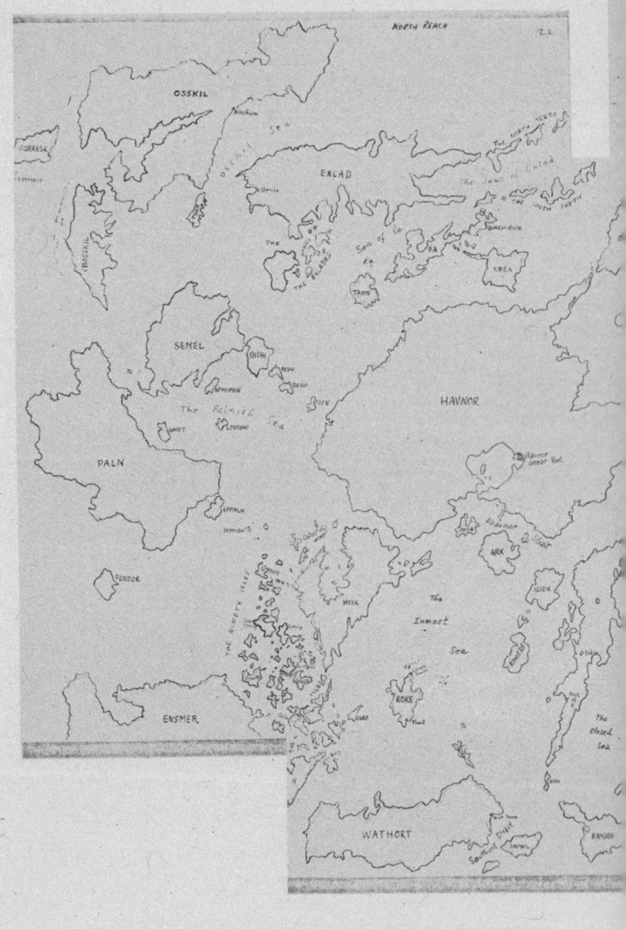
NORTH REACH
22
OSSKIL
FORRESK
EBOSKIL
ENLAD
The Jaws of Enlad
THE NORTH TEETH
THE SOUTH TEETH
Sea of Ea
EA
EBSA
TAON
THE ENLADES
SEMEL
OSSKIL SEA
The Paln? Sea
HAVNOR
PALN
PENDOR
THE NINETY ISLES
MOSK
The Inmost Sea
ROKE
ARK
ILIEN
ENSMER
The Closed Sea
WATHORT
Southing Strait
Ebavnor Strait
Havnor Great Port

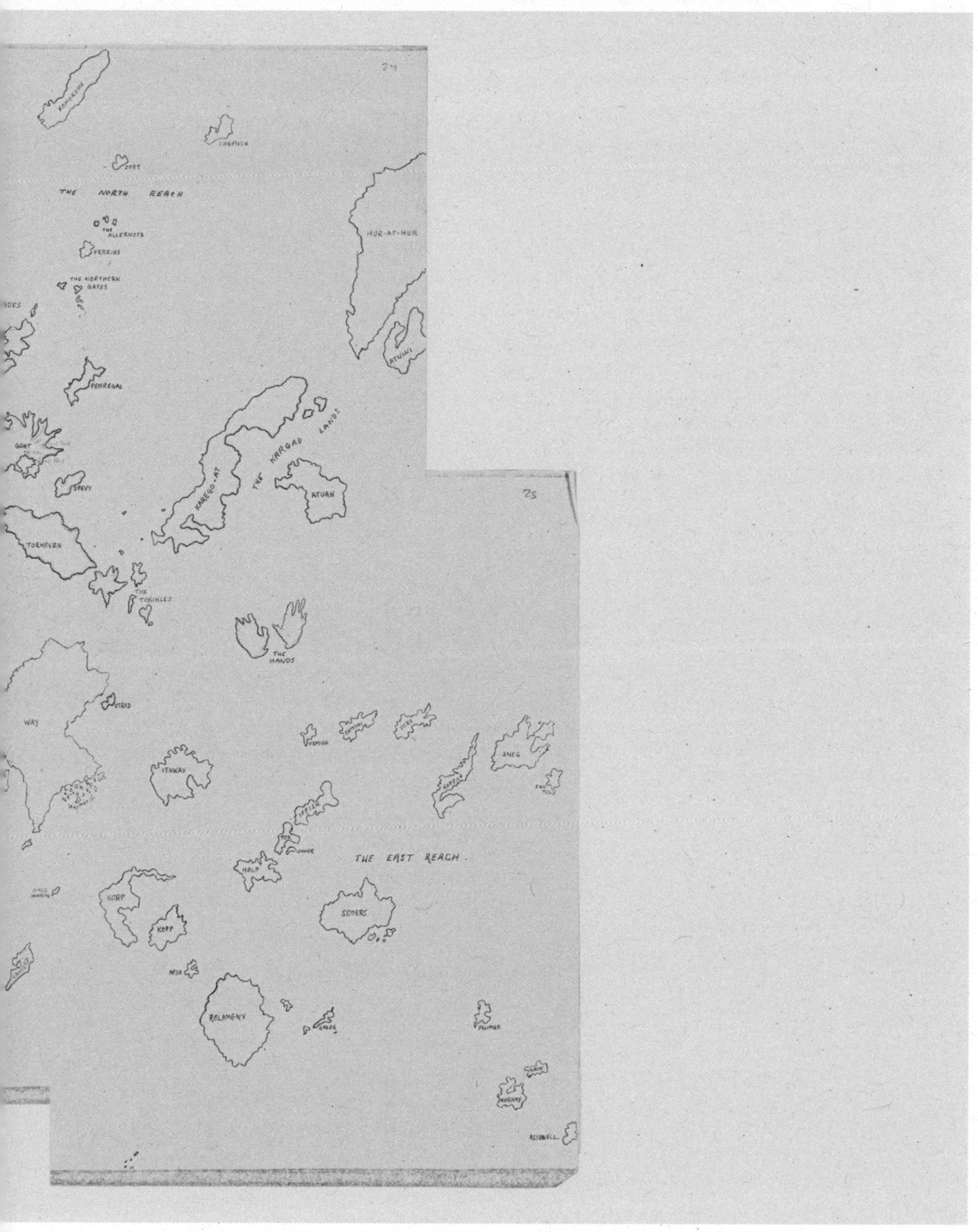

Composite drawing of Earthsea, unpublished, for *A Wizard of Earthsea* (1968).

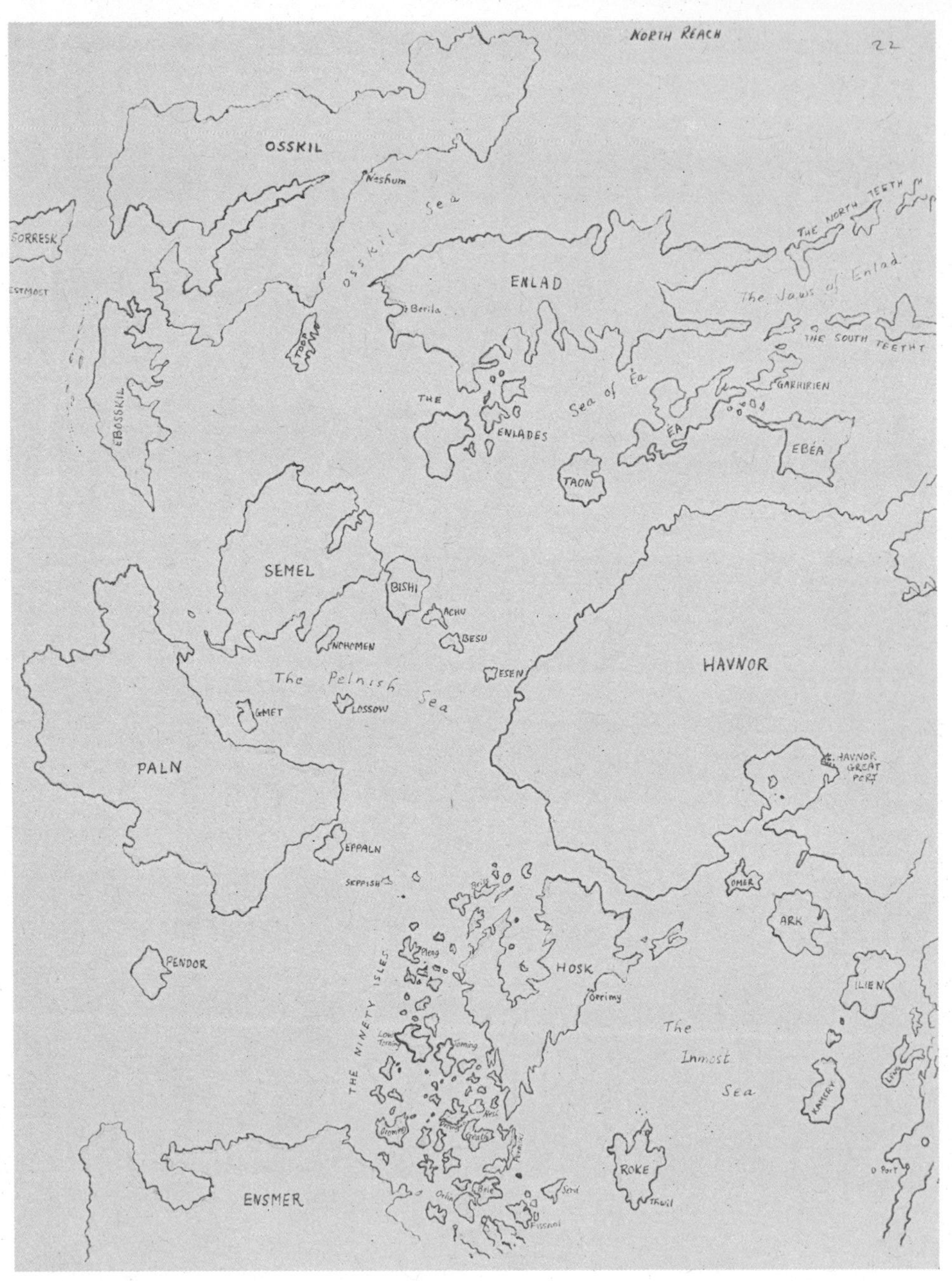

West-central Earthsea, unpublished, for *A Wizard of Earthsea* (1968).

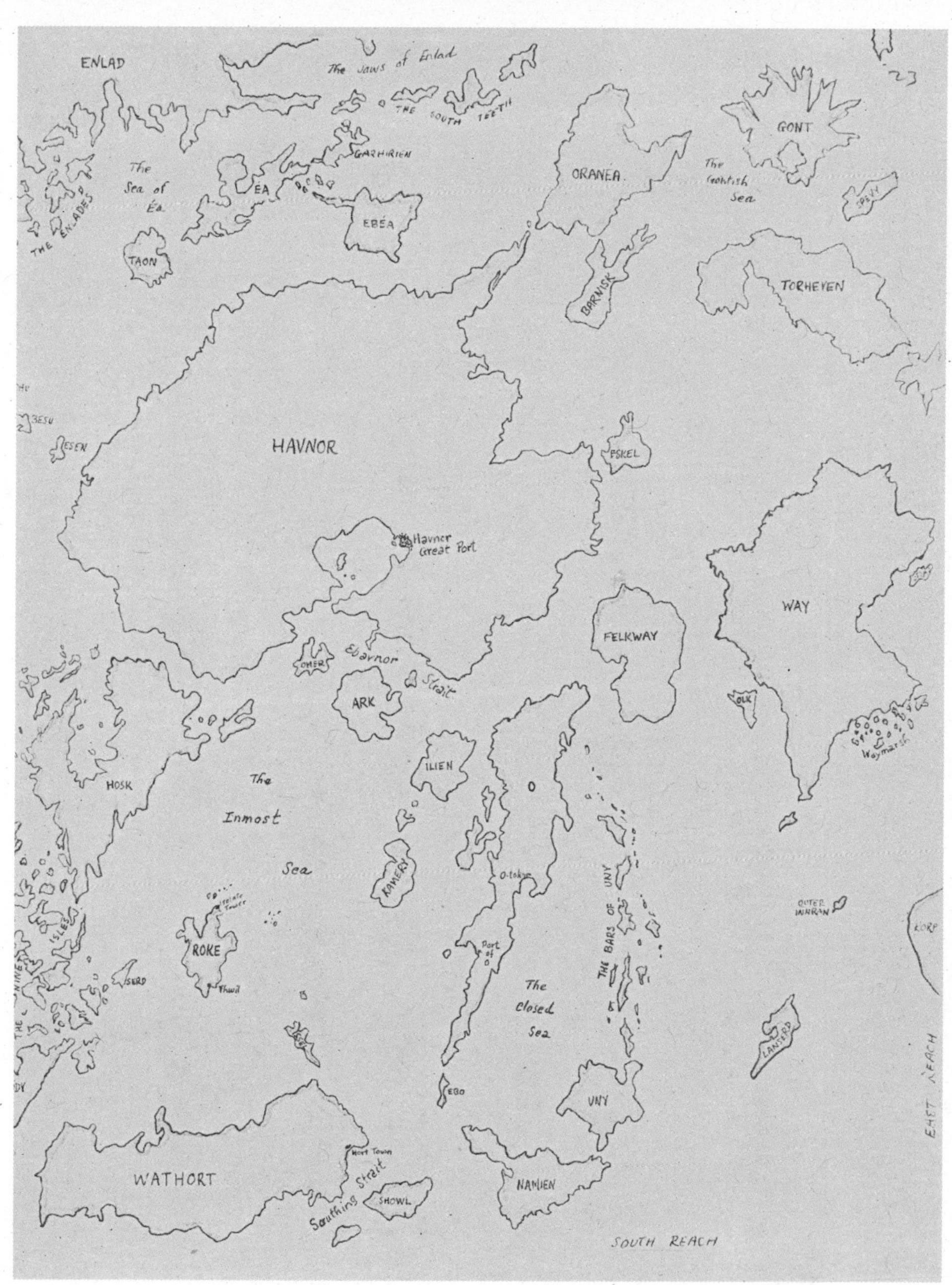

East and central Earthsea, unpublished, for *A Wizard of Earthsea* (1968).

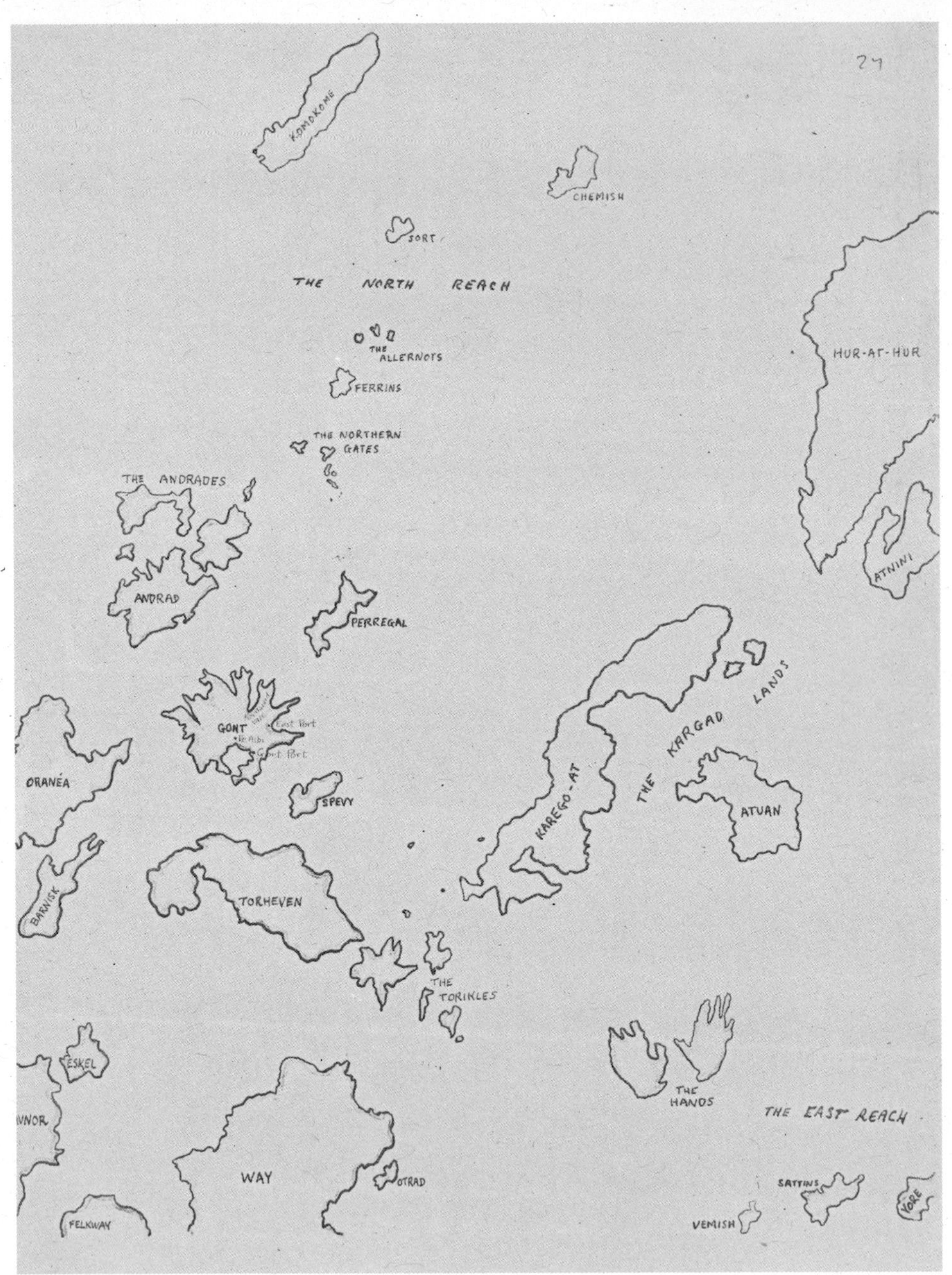

Northeast Earthsea, unpublished,
for *A Wizard of Earthsea* (1968).

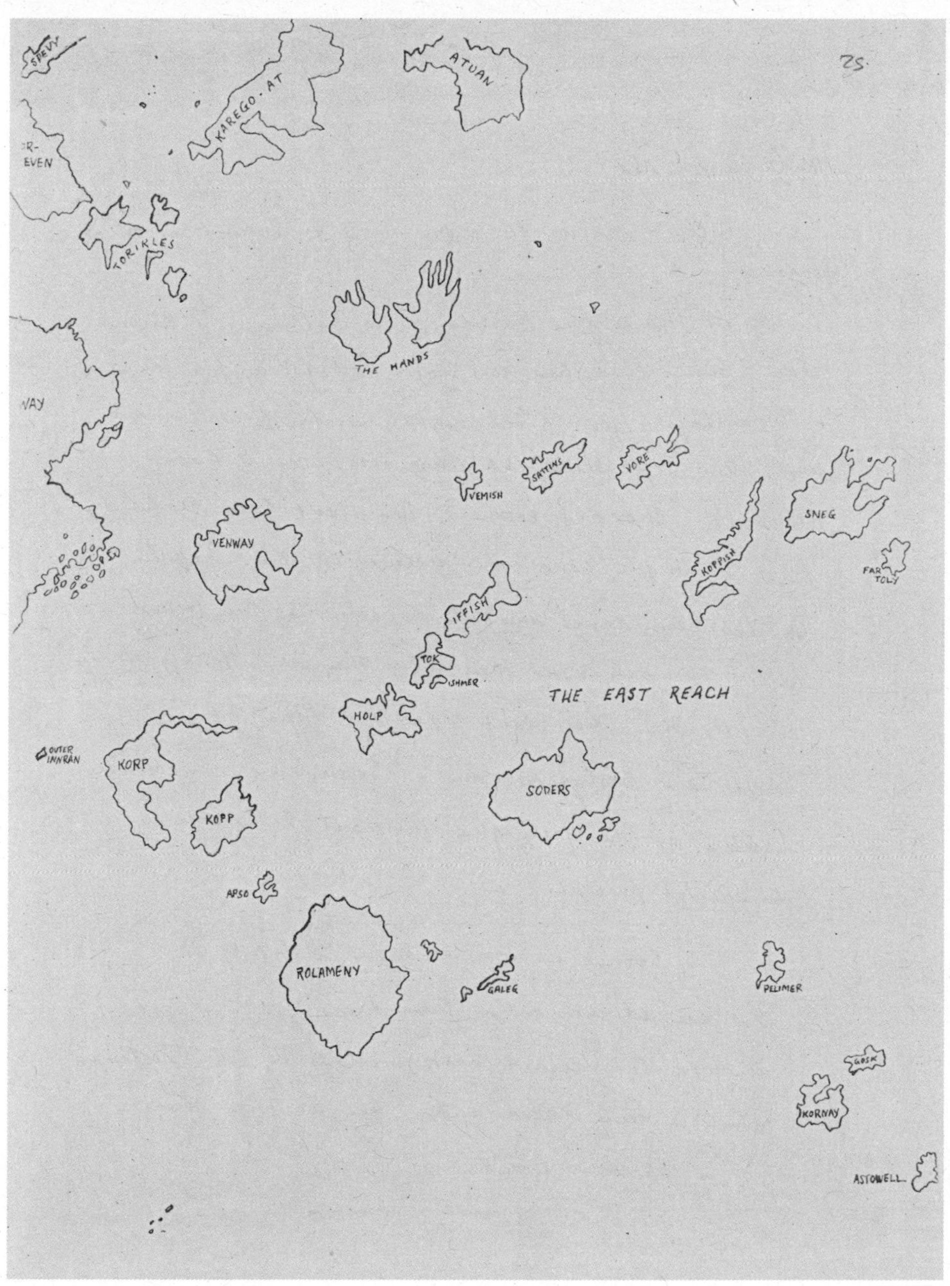

Southeast Earthsea, unpublished,
for *A Wizard of Earthsea* (1968).

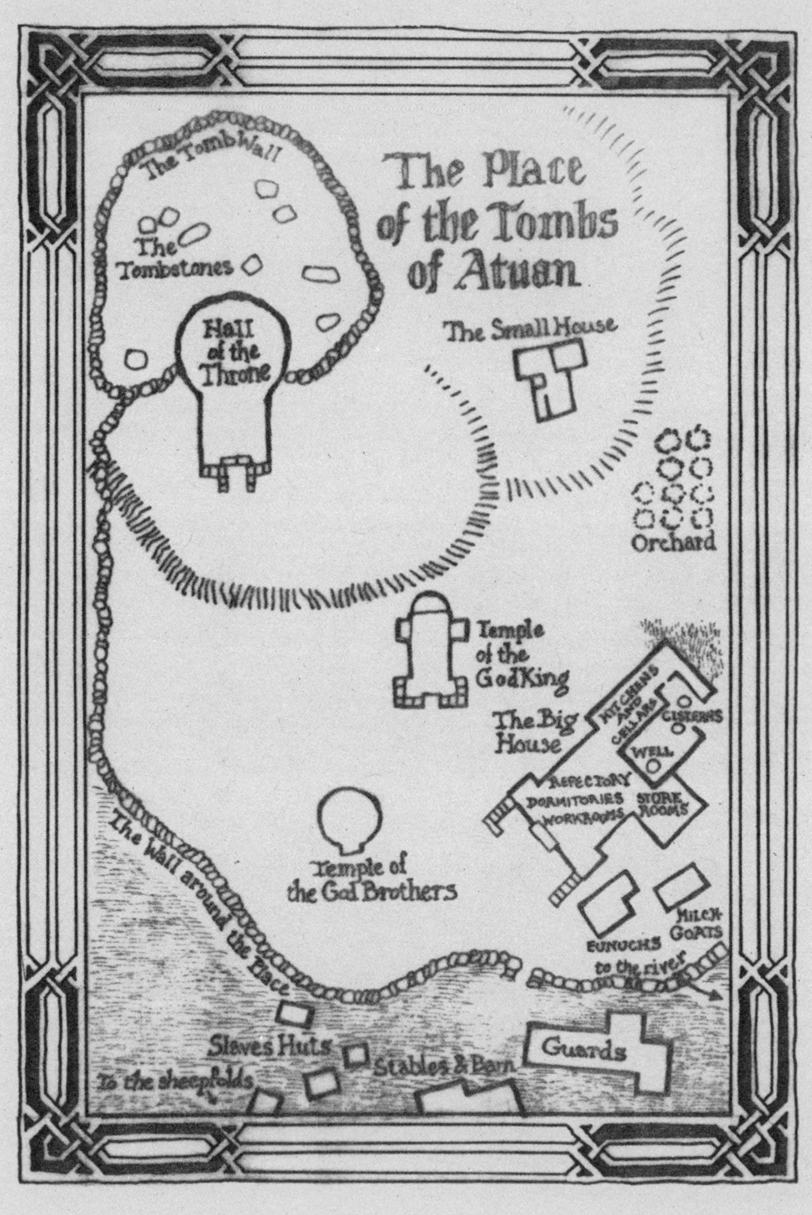

The Place of the Tombs of Atuan,
published in *The Tombs of Atuan* (1970).

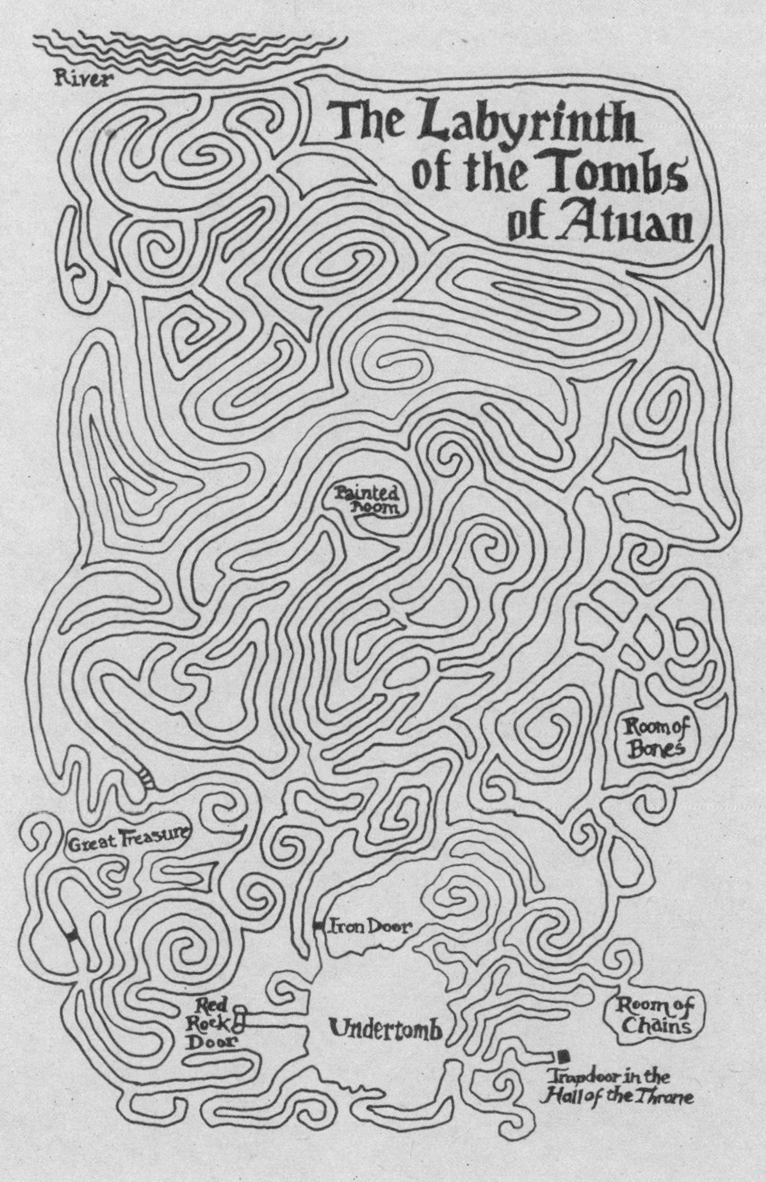

The Labyrinth of the Tombs of Atuan,
published in *The Tombs of Atuan* (1970).

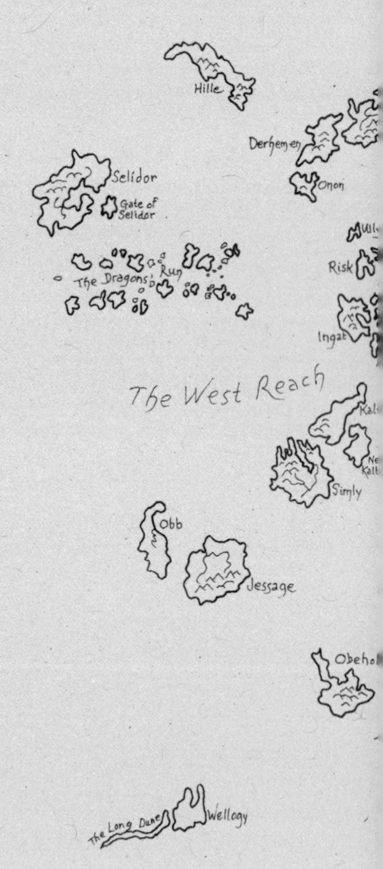
Hille
Derhemen
Selidor
Gate of Selidor
Onon
Risk
The Dragons' Run
Ingat
The West Reach
Simly
Obb
Jessage
The Long Dune
Wellogy

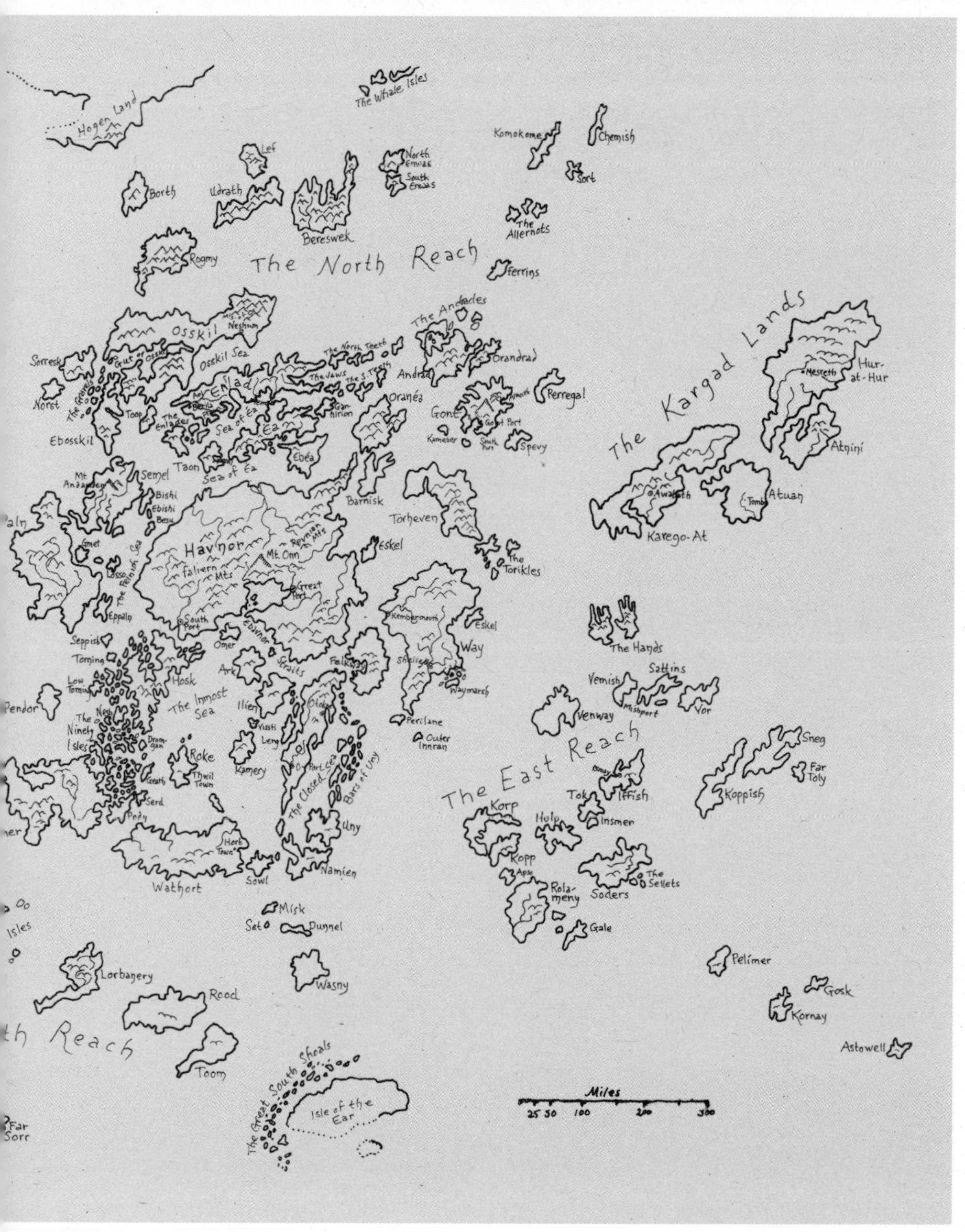

Earthsea, for the Watershed Center.

Theo Downes-Le Guin

The Geography of Imagination

My mother described herself as uneasy with abstraction. Though her writing is scaffolded by concepts of gender, power and progress, and though she used literary abstraction such as metaphor throughout her work, the symbolic and formal systems of mathematics and logic felt alien and uncomfortable to her. Ursula's preferred form of abstraction, the one at which she excelled, was imagination. Imagination was not, for her, abstract, which is why the worlds she imagined do not feel abstract to readers. And within her imagination, Ursula carved out an exception for cartography – a form of symbolic abstraction, to be sure, but one that worked for her.

Cartography formed an early and integral part of her writing process. Maps acted as a tool to create specificity and consistency within Ursula's inventions, a realism for places that aren't real. Early in her writing life, Ursula's prose was set in realistic places that don't quite exist, like Orsinia, which looks a lot like – but isn't exactly – Eastern Europe. Her cartography and writing codeveloped more easily within semi-realism. Jumping into a visual articulation of a completely imagined place like Earthsea or the planet Werel would challenge any young writer. Mirroring her early realism, for her final novel *Lavinia* (2008) Ursula mapped the Latium region of modern Italy to verify that a walk she described as taking three days could actually be done in that time. Whether mapping Latium or a distant planet, the point was to define rules for her stories, lending them credibility and a sense of truthfulness. A sentiment she expressed regarding her preference for book illustrations summarises the role she wanted her maps to play: to create 'a strong, vivid, striking realism. Not a fanciful dreamworld, but an imaginary world accurately drawn and vividly, intensely seen. A world real people live in, and real dragons.'[1]

Some theorists might see this quest for accuracy as a version of 'all fiction is lies': in other words, that cartography is used in an attempt to convince readers of places, time and people that don't exist. Ursula did refer to fiction as a form of lying from time to time, but only playfully, in her mode of author as Coyote trickster. In her formal reflections on the nature of fantasy, she was punctilious about drawing distinctions between fiction and lies, as in a 2013 festival talk (later revised for publication in *Words Are My Matter*), in which she said, 'Fiction is invention, but it is not lies. It moves on a different level of reality from either fact-finding or lying ... Imagination, even in its wildest flights, is not detached from reality: imagination acknowledges reality, starts from it, and returns to it to enrich it.'[2]

I can only speculate on the early development of Ursula's cartographic skills. From childhood, she was a gifted draftsperson, though she never aspired to more than amateur status. Her drawings, sketches, pastels and cartoons evince a natural gift for two-dimensional spatial imagining. She also absorbed the habits of her anthropologist and writer parents, helping her father to map sites mentioned in the song-cycles of Indigenous people he worked with, and to calculate distances between these sites.[3] In the way she used maps I can't help but see a reflection of how her father's generation of scientists placed great faith in the connection between measurement and enlightenment. Recently I reread my grandfather's 1919 study of how cultural phenomena might behave according to predictable cycles. He based his analysis on data points of women's fashion – such as skirt length – during a 76-year period, inferred and recorded from fashion plates. Read against modern standards, it seems like a naïve stab at a grand unifying theory based on a tiny dataset. In historical context, however, I see a brilliant social scientist's attempt to extend from imagination to symbolic data, and from data to profound understanding – a quest for what Ursula described as the realism of a larger reality.

The strongest family influence might, however, have been the Napa Valley ranch her parents bought in 1930. Here the centrality of the map in Ursula's life connects to something broader, to ideas of home and place prevalent throughout her writing. Ursula identified deeply and forever as a person of the western United

States. She inhabited three main places in her life: her childhood home in Berkeley, California (1929–47); her adult home in Portland, Oregon (1960–2018); and through it all, the ranch (1930–2018). Until her final trip in 2016, Ursula spent the entirety of her childhood summers, and weeks or months of almost every year as an adult, roaming the ranch's 35 acres of pasture, forest and creeks with complete freedom. There she was taught to write, or at least to form letters, by her brother Ted. There she drew countless sketches of trees, hills and structures *en plein air*. Until her death she could map those acres' contours and details from memory. Some version of that ranch courses through nearly all her writing, most explicitly in *Always Coming Home* (1985), but gently and subtly in other books, stories and poems. The landscape's topography, imprinted on her more or less at birth, is her ur-map, at once real, remembered and imagined.

Among the maps she drew for books, Ursula was most often asked about the map for the first edition of *A Wizard of Earthsea* (1968). In her introduction to *The Books of Earthsea*, she wrote:

> ... the first thing I did was sit down and draw a map. I saw and named Earthsea and all its islands. I knew almost nothing about them, but I knew their names. In the name is the magic. The original map was on a very large sheet – probably butcher paper, which I had rolls of for my kids to draw on ... Its use to me was practical. A navigator needs a chart. As my characters sailed about, I needed to know how far apart the islands lay and in which direction one from another.[4]

This description of the practical and navigational uses of the Earthsea map echoes Tolkien's description of how he fitted Middle-earth to his map, rather than fitting his map to Middle-earth. My mother's map also aligns broadly with the aesthetics of Tolkien's. The two authors have distinct styles, but both created maps which are cartographic and also illustrative, and which evoke an out-of-time feel that now universally connotes Fantasy.

Tolkien's influence on Ursula's maps is indisputable but not unique. Linguist and publisher Michael Everson recently noted a small map of the island of Saint Helena, the site of Napoleon's final exile, which my parents likely picked up in the early 1950s at a Parisian *marché aux puces* (flea market), and which hung in their house for a half-century. The map could easily pass for an island of Earthsea in its shape and style of mountain-shading. (Perhaps, given that the map was printed in the 17th century, I should say that Ursula's Earthsea could easily pass for an archipelago made up of many Saint Helenas.) I don't think this represents Ursula's cartographic Rosebud; indeed I don't think there is a Rosebud for Ursula, or for Earthsea. Instead, I think the map – along with Tolkien and myriad other influences – was in her subconscious as she drew. In any case, that first map of Earthsea, though magnificent, is *sui generis* in Ursula's output. Elsewhere, her use of maps is, as with her stories, more spiral than linear, and primarily for herself rather than for readers.

The majority of the non-Earthsea maps are workmanlike, described by Ursula as 'research ... into the geography of my own imagination'. In her science fiction and realist fiction, she adopted a simple and contemporary style. Her maps of Urras and Anarres for *The Dispossessed* (1974) are relatively bare-boned, more a visual reminder of the separation of planet and moon than a key to understanding the narrative. Most editions of this book use Ursula's little planet and moon drawings mainly as chapter headings to cue the reader to a change in setting. Similarly, her maps for *Searoad* (1991) render a detailed but less decorative topography of an imagined coastal town – a town very similar to the one in which my parents had a weekend house, in which several local topographic maps hung, and in which she wrote most of the book. Many of these maps wound up in books after being modified or entirely redrawn by their publishers. This didn't bother Ursula; she loved cartographer collaborations, learned from them, and revised her own maps as a result of what she learned. For my part, publishers' preferences for making a hand-drawn and hand-lettered map more polished is mystifying. Maps are so personal, as personal as words, and I don't enjoy seeing another person's aesthetic overlaid on my mother's.

My mother worked hard to make her unrealities realistic, harder than many literary fiction writers work to make their realism realistic. Books set in real places, accurately and vividly described, aren't uncommon in any era. But in my estimation, contemporary literary fiction often relies too heavily on brand names, references to current events, or descriptions of characters' small-difference narcissisms to inject a feeling of place and moment. As for an actual map, lovingly drawn by the writer and reproduced by the publisher? This seems nearly unthinkable for books aspiring to literary fiction status. Of course, readers can always find a map of a real place on their own initiative, but I don't think this is the reason we see so few maps in contemporary realism. Somewhere along the way, maps – like illustrations – came to signify less-than-literary. Fantasy and science fiction writers, who even now are accustomed to this kind of genre bias, can't rely on presumed familiarity or on shorthand descriptions for their inventions. They must create a place whole cloth and bring it to life with nothing but words and the occasional map or picture. How fortunate for us that they do.

Theo Downes-Le Guin
Portland, Oregon
June 2025

1 Le Guin's notes to artist David Lupton for the Folio Society's Books of Earthsea, quoted in part in the Folio Society blog, 'A Celebration of Ursula K Le Guin', 14 June 2022, https://www.foliosociety.com/uk/blog/this-folio-life-a-celebration-of-ursula-k-le-guin.

2 Le Guin, 'Making Up Stories', in *Words Are My Matter: Writing About Life and Books 2000-2016* (Small Beer Press, 2016), p 108.

3 Dell Hymes, 'A Native American Epic', in *Folklore Fellows Network Bulletin* 20, November 2000.

4 Le Guin, 'Introduction', in *The Books of Earthsea: The Complete Illustrated Edition* (Gollancz, 2018), p ix.

David Naimon

Mapping the Inland Sea:

Landlines and Waterways

As I wonder and wander my way towards what Ursula K Le Guin's relationship to maps and mapping might be, the first thing that comes to mind is her 1986 commencement speech given at the all-women's Bryn Mawr College in Pennsylvania. In it, she says to the new graduates:

> If being a cog in the machine or a puppet manipulated by others isn't what you want, you can find out what you want, your needs, desires, truths, powers, by accepting your own experience as a woman, as this woman, this body, this person, your hungry self. On the maps drawn by men there is an immense white area, terra incognita, where most women live. That country is all yours to explore, to inhabit, to describe.[1]

Nine South American women enact this suggestion quite literally within Le Guin's 1982 short story 'Sur: A Summer Report of the Yelcho Expedition to the Antarctic'. Presented as an unpublished true testimony (and who's to say it isn't one?), it recounts how the women tell their friends and family they are going to Paris or into a Bolivian convent for the six months of their absence. Instead, they sail together from Chile to that 'immense white area' on the map, Antarctica, where they dig out a base and begin a gruelling expedition to the South Pole. The many challenges they run into – from blizzards and snow blindness to the inopportune discovery that one of them is not only pregnant, but due to give birth before their return to the ship – do not prevent them from becoming the first expedition to make it to the South Pole, getting there several years before its official discovery in 1911 by Roald Amundsen and his all-male team. But most notably, these women decide not to plant a flag, not to tell the world, not to mark the map or 'make history'. They go 'to see – no more, no less' and leave the place 'fresh' for future experience.[2]

Thinking of both this speech and Le Guin's story (or secret testimony) as dual headwaters for this piece, it would be remiss not to mention that prior to meeting Ursula in person for the first time, I met her through her own beloved terra incognita.

That year, wildfire season in the Pacific Northwest had scuttled my plans to hike in the North Cascades and I was scrambling to find an alternative. I was scheduled some months later to interview Le Guin about her book *Steering the Craft: A Twenty-First-Century Guide to Sailing the Sea of Story*. I was to pick her up at her house in Portland, Oregon, nestled near the entrance to one the largest urban forests in the United States. And I confess, though I wasn't nervous about interviewing her, I was nervous about picking her up and making small talk in my rundown ancient Volvo beforehand. Knowing of Le Guin's longstanding love of the Steens Mountain region in the remote high desert of southeastern Oregon, somewhere I had never been, I gave her a call – for guidance, but also to break the ice.

Excited to come to my aid, she set me up with the people she usually stayed with, in a town whose welcome sign read 'population 5' with the five superimposed upon a still-legible seven beneath. I mention the population because Harney County, where Steens Mountain sits, is not only the largest county in Oregon but also the least densely populated. You can drive for hours and see far more antelope, raptors and coyote than people or cars. As in many fantasy novels, humans and our creations are dwarfed by the scope and majesty of the landscape itself, just one small element within it. There are so few people in southeastern Oregon that it contains the largest 'dark sky' sanctuary in the world. A misnomer, if there ever was one, as in the absence of human light the skies there are illuminated scrolls: three-dimensional, alive and signifying.

These fifth-generation ranchers welcomed me as a 'friend of Ursula', someone I had yet to meet but whom they clearly considered one of them (Le Guin's own family had tried to homestead in this region before moving back to California). They knew her not through her books, or as a writer, but as a birdwatcher, a sky watcher, a contemplator, a person easily knitted into the same world whose fabric they themselves were part of.

We can glean great insight about Le Guin's own relationship to this place from her introduction to *Out Here* (2010), a collection of her poetry and sketches juxtaposed with the landscape photography of Roger Dorband and dedicated 'to all our friends in Harney County, with love.' In that foreword she states that not only is the entire American West seen by people in the eastern United States as 'out there', but that the population centres of Oregon's western valleys also saw this remote high desert to its east as 'out there' too. 'And that's as it should be,' Le Guin continues. 'It really is somewhere else...And yet, once you get here, it's as here as a place can be: landscape that is immensely and intensely vivid, present. But still, it's *out* here. Distance is inherent in its presence.'[3] This revelatory inversion of 'out there' to 'out here' rhymes with the inversion she makes in the Bryn Mawr speech, where the immense white areas on maps drawn by men become the here-ness, the centre, for the active generative work of the female imagination. Those same uncharted spaces were once marked 'here be dragons'.

***

In 2005, a collection of scholarly essays was published, *The New Utopian Politics of Ursula K. Le Guin's The Dispossessed*, with an afterword by Le Guin herself. There, she expressed how much she had learned about her own work through the writers' reflections on it. She did lament, however, that so many of them treated *The Dispossessed* ahistorically as a stand-alone self-contained work when, in her mind, it wasn't an anomaly within her writing life. In fact, she suggests, many of the elements in that novel are carried a great deal further a decade later in *Always Coming Home*.

Le Guin was mainly referring to elements of narrative experimentation and post-modern fictional techniques here. For all its indelible radical imaginings,

The Dispossessed is formally quite traditional: a comparison of two societies, one capitalist, one anarcho-syndicalist, seen through the eyes and consciousness of one remarkable protagonist, the physicist Shevek. *Always Coming Home*, on the other hand, becomes radical in form as well as content. Imagined as 'an archaeology of the future', it is replete with maps, songs, stories, recipes and rituals, all of which radically decentre the individual on behalf of a collective, multimodal and multinodal form of storytelling. But I want to suggest a deep and longstanding philosophical journey coming to full fruition in *Always Coming Home* as well: one related to place and land and the human role within it, and one that deeply speaks to Le Guin's relationship to maps and mapping, with the maps in *Always Coming Home* as the best example of her worldview in full bloom.

To understand how she travels from *The Dispossessed* to *Always Coming Home* – from the 'out there' of a settler-colony on a rebel moon, one that only marginally supports human life, to the 'out here' of an Indigenous community in an ecologically diverse and flourishing post-apocalyptic California – isn't to look at Le Guin's relationship to terra incognita, whether the terra incognita of Harney County, Antarctica or Anarres. Instead, I think we must look, as she does, to water.

Shortly after Donald Trump was first elected President of the United States in November 2016, Le Guin shared her 119th blog post, 'The Election, Lao Tzu, a Cup of Water'. In it, she wonders how to resist, and is deeply sceptical of mirroring the aggression of the Trump administration. 'We have glamorized the way of the warrior for millennia,' she says. 'We have identified it as the supreme test and example of courage, strength, duty, generosity and manhood. If I turn from the way of the warrior, where am I to seek those qualities? What way have I to go? Lao Tzu says: the way of water.'[4]

She then explores the character of water in the *Tao Te Ching*, a text she describes elsewhere as 'the most lovable of all the great religious texts, funny, keen, kind, modest, indestructibly outrageous, and inexhaustibly refreshing. Of all the deep springs, this is the purest water. To me, it is also the deepest spring.'[5] But strangely, in a meditation on resistance – whether in Selma or Standing Rock or to the tyranny of Trump's presidency – the essay speaks of water's laudatory qualities as those of weakness. Of water as yielding, offering no resistance, accepting whatever comes. And of the immense power of that obedience.

Yes, there is an incredible power within water's patience: a substance that seems to assume the shape of everything it encounters, but over time is the one doing the shaping. But what of obedience? And what, if we follow the way of water, are we supposed to be obedient to?

To me, the answer to this question is the key to understanding the journey Le Guin took between *The Dispossessed* and *Always Coming Home*. European anarchism and Indigenous lifeways share many qualities: no government, no police, no coercion. They emphasise mutual aid and solidarity horizontally between peoples. *The Dispossessed* explores the ambiguous utopia of just such a world. But in Indigenous worldviews such as the one that emerges through *Always Coming Home*, you are beholden to a superstructure of sorts, to the pull of the earth, to nature itself, and the reciprocity it demands of us to stay in right relationship with it. Or, as Ursula puts it, water models a 'steady obedience to necessity.'

Le Guin's model of water resonates with the Indigenous framework proposed by the Michi Saagiig Nishnaabeg writer and scholar Leanne Betasamosake Simpson in her 2025 book *Theory of Water: Nishnaabe Maps to the Times Ahead*. Simpson speaks of water as iterative, resilient, interdependent, transformative, decentralised and always creating more possibilities. It is within us and connects us to all forms of life. And in that spirit, she speaks less of *making* worlds with humans as central protagonists, and more of knitting ourselves *into* the world, woven in mutual consent alongside plants and animals doing the same. She speaks of a process called sintering which snow undergoes when the temperature is below freezing. When a snowflake joins the snowpack and sinters, it retains its distinctiveness as it joins the other snowflakes, weaving itself into and bonding with the existing environment without destroying its neighbours. Sintered snow remains and endures long after other snow has melted.[6]

In *Always Coming Home*, the maps frequently toggle between those with place names (p 53) and those without (p 52). But in both cases, you feel the prominence of water, the distinct architecture of a watershed as the map's skeleton, the human names and human settlements knitted within and modelled after the immense power of water's obedience.

The city Ursula and I both called home – Portland, Oregon – has a long and deep history of radical left-wing activism including anarchism, a strong DIY ethos and an emphasis on mutual aid. And yet none of this radicalism, when set within a settler-colonial framework, necessitates a reciprocal relationship to the land or a consideration of water. The city where this all occurs is built upon an immense wetland that once, in precolonial times, was mainly a place to forage and hunt rather than a place to live. It is a place whose wetlands were filled with rocks and trash, its springs and innumerable streams and creeks diverted underground, so the city grid could be established without considering them. The thriving future indigeneity in *Always Coming Home*'s California imagines an otherwise that would.

The people in this world – the Kesh – like to draw maps, and often carry them with them. But since these people knew their world so intimately, 'from mountains to molehills', their maps served less as guides than as talismans. And interestingly, the talismanic maps are shown without the place names, with the topography itself almost bursting with inherent magic (p 61).

Le Guin says of the maps made in this world: 'The larger maps were remarkably accurate, considering that their function was mostly aesthetic or poetic; but then, accuracy was considered a fundamental element or quality of poetry.' Thinking of maps as primarily not for orientation, but rather for something fundamentally beyond utility – an art, a protection, a mystery – reminds me of the first conflict in *Always Coming Home*. A conflict about technology, where the more warlike people want to build a bridge for quicker, more efficient crossing of their men. The others argue there is already a crossing farther down, and that is more than enough. It may seem strange to think of a bridge as technology but when Ursula and I first talked, she argued that the kitchen knife was a perfect technology, and that technology is not only or even mainly high-tech. Rather, it is 'how society copes with physical reality'; technology as the 'active human interface with the material world'.

Perhaps this is why human place names rest so lightly on the maps of the Kesh, to underscore that it is the land, the material world, which is primary. And much of high-tech, the result of our desire for speed, efficiency and convenience, is supported by massive exploitation of that very world, as if that world were limitless and asked nothing of us in return. And really, in this increasingly extractive high-tech world, what were the odds that when I called Ursula, and later called her friends in Harney County, that all this would happen from one nearly obsolete landline to the next to the next, phones with cords tethering each of us to our nearby walls? It was enough, more than enough, to talk and connect this way.

In *Always Coming Home*, maps within the Valley always take the principal creek as their axis: the source of the stream is the top of the map, and the maps are oriented to the flow of water, with 'down' as the bottom of the page. Perhaps water is what connects Le Guin's engagement with feminism, anarchism, Taoism, indigeneity and place. Perhaps to model oneself and one's inner and outer maps on water is the essence of Out Hereness – not to make a mark on a map or on history, but to recognise water as the ultimate mapmaker, to submit to the mystery that water models both resistance and coexistence, to weave oneself into this map of the world drawn not by human hands, to come 'to see – no more, no less', to sinter oneself into a landscape and sky-scape so immense and alive it could swallow you – and it does – like a dragon.

'The death way or the life way?' Ursula asks. 'The high road of the warrior, or the river road?'[7]

1 Le Guin, 'Bryn Mawr Commencement Address (1986)', in *Space Crone*, edited by So Mayer and Sarah Shin (Silver Press, 2023), p 43.

2 Le Guin, 'Sur', in *Space Crone*, p 8.

3 Le Guin, 'Foreword', in *Out Here: Poems and Images from Steens Mountain Country, with* photographs by Roger Dorband (Raven Studios, 2010), p 10.

4 Le Guin, 'The Election, Lao Tzu, a Cup of Water', November 2016. https://www.ursulakleguin.com/blog/119-the-election-lao-tzu-a-cup-of-water.

5 Le Guin, 'Introduction', in *Lao Tzu: Tao Te Ching* (Shambhala, 2019), p x.

6 Leanne Betasamosake Simpson, *Theory of Water: Nishnaabe Maps to the Times Ahead* (Haymarket, 2025), pp 17–8.

7 Le Guin, 'The Election, Lao Tzu, a Cup of Water'.

Restoring Shoshone Ancestral Foods Gathering Group

Buffalo Stew

Restoring Shoshone Ancestral Foods Gathering (RSAFG) is a grassroots community group in what is now called the state of Wyoming, United States. RSAFG comes together in the reclamation of ancestral foods and the promotion of food sovereignty and Land Back. Our work embodies equity, decolonisation and community empowerment, showing how the Shoshone People are connected and have belonged to the land in so-called Wyoming, Idaho, Utah and beyond for thousands of years.

This map, made collectively by RSAFG, represents more than geography. It is a living testament to the ancestral lands of the Shoshone People – lands that have provided Original Instruction for thousands of years, including food, medicine and knowledge. This map is an act of Indigenous counter-mapping, a process that overwrites colonial mapping techniques whose fixed boundaries and place names dispossess original inhabitants. A method of withdrawing the colonial lens, it seeks to restore Shoshone presence to the landscape, reaffirms Shoshone sovereignty and strengthens the 1863 and 1868 Fort Bridger Treaty rights. The map re-places the plant and animal peoples that collectively come together in buffalo stew on a topographical representation of land to show how intimately peoples and place are entwined in everything we do.

Recipe:
Buffalo Stew
Yield: ~6 1-cup servings

Ingredients:

1 pound buffalo meat (round or chuck)
6 cups water
1 cup cattail stalk or roots, chopped
1 cup sego lily bulbs
½ cup wild onion, chopped
½ cup yampah root, chopped
1 cup biscuitroot meal
½ cup chokecherries, pitted
½ cup camas, chopped
½ cup fireweed, chopped or shredded
½ cup bitterroot, chopped or shredded
Birch sap and/or serviceberries (to taste; offsets the bitterroot)
Salt bush (to taste; flavour enhancer)

Equipment needed:

Two-quart saucepan
Cutting board
Chef's knife
Large serving spoon

Cooking Instructions:

1. Place buffalo meat in two-quart saucepan.
2. Add water to two inches above the meat.
3. Cook over medium heat for two hours.
4. Add cattail, sego lily bulbs, wild onion, yampah root, biscuitroot meal/flour, chokecherries, camas, fireweed, bitterroot, birch sap and/or serviceberries.
5. Continue cooking, stirring regularly, until the stew has thickened (about 20–30 minutes).
6. Store in a container.
7. Place in refrigerator, ensuring internal temperature is less than 41°F within four hours.
8. Reheat until internal temperature is 165°F.

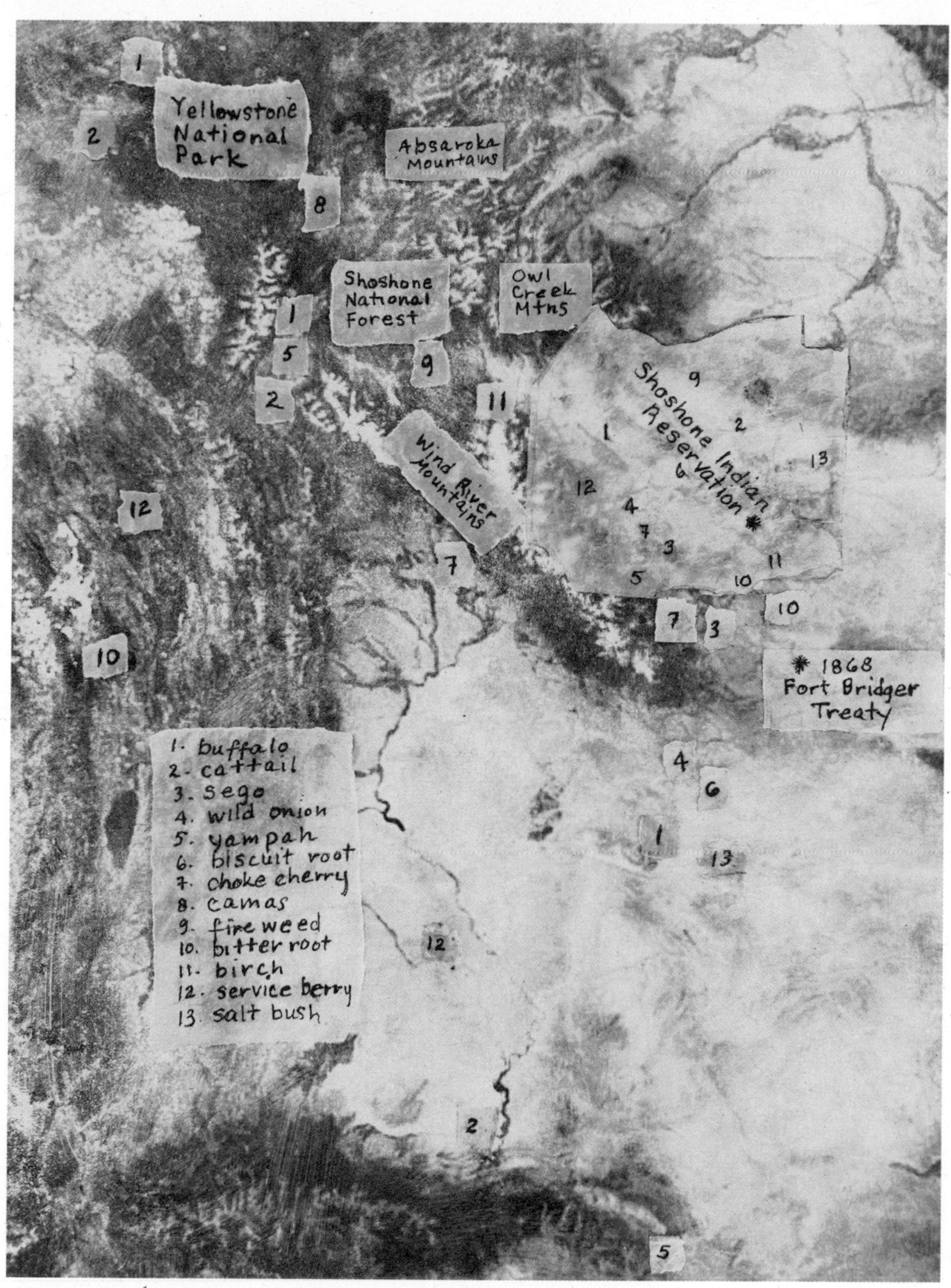
1
Yellowstone National Park
2
Absaroka Mountains
8
Shoshone National Forest
Owl Creek Mtns
1
5
9
2
11
Shoshone Indian Reservation
9
1
2
13
6
12
4
7
3
5
10
11
Wind River Mountains
12
7
7
3
10
10
* 1868 Fort Bridger Treaty
1. buffalo
2. cattail
3. sego
4. wild onion
5. yampah
6. biscuit root
7. choke cherry
8. camas
9. fire weed
10. bitter root
11. birch
12. service berry
13. salt bush
4
6
1
13
12
2
5

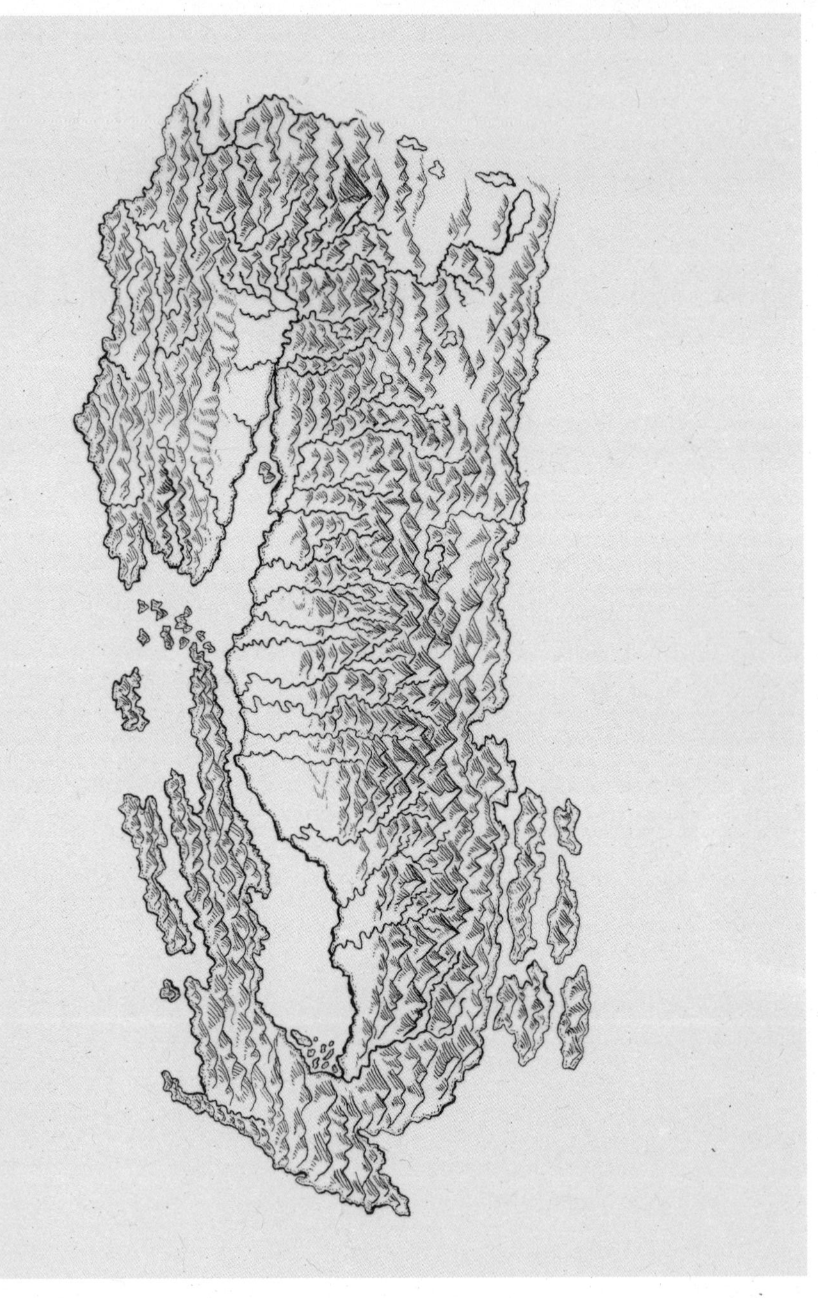

The Rivers That Run into the Inland Sea, published in *Always Coming Home* (1985).

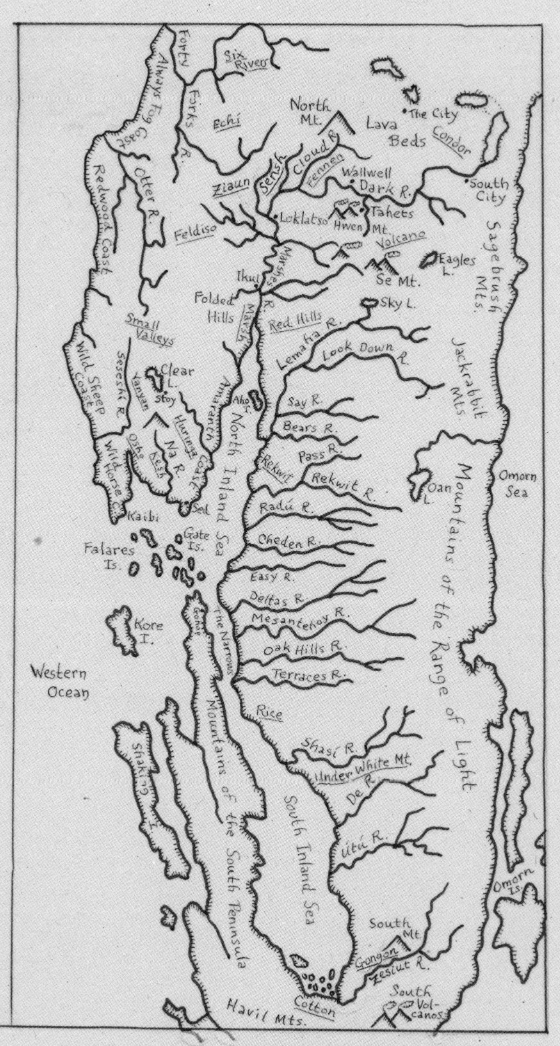

Some of the People and Places Known to the Kesh, published in *Always Coming Home* (1985).

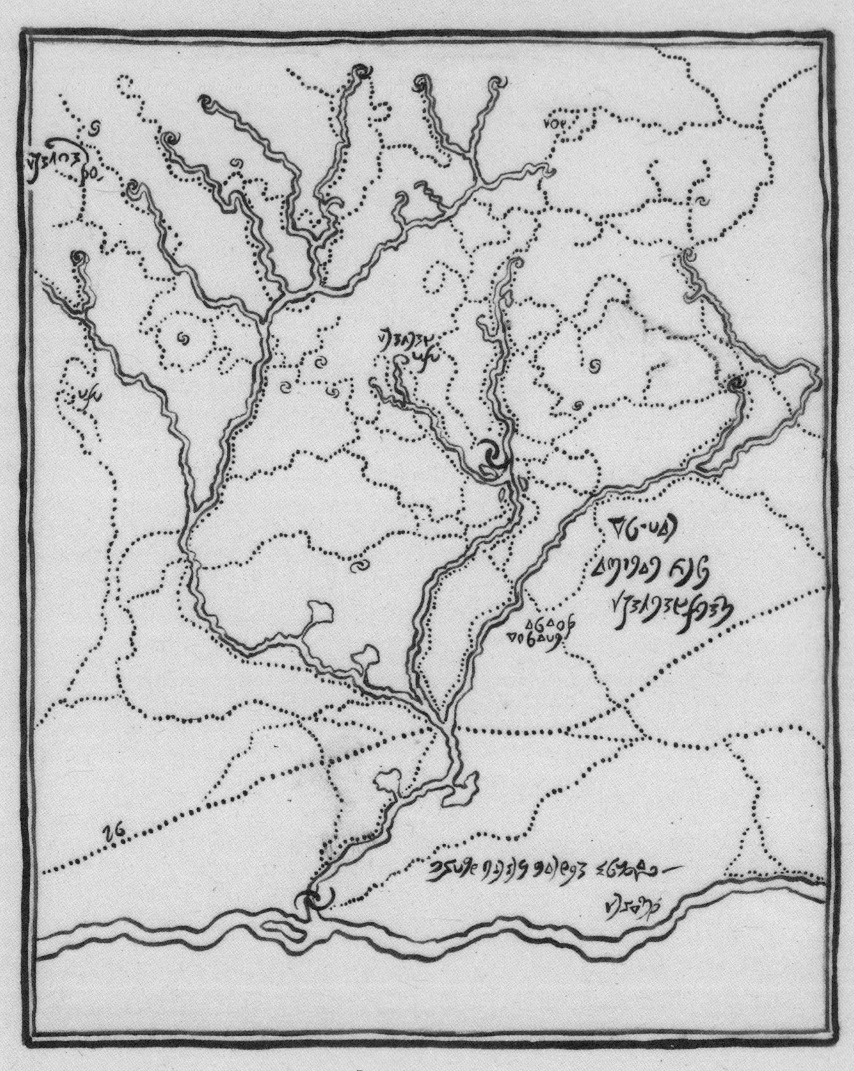

Some of the Paths around Sinshan Creek, published in *Always Coming Home* (1985).

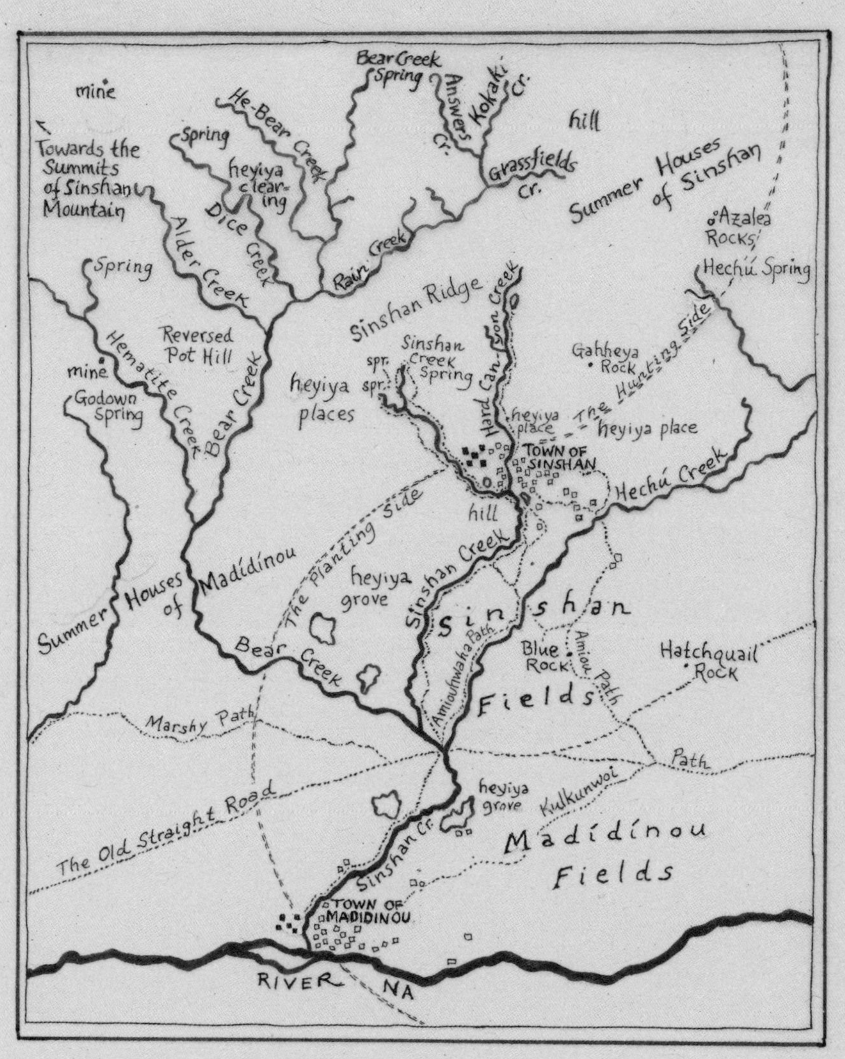

The Watershed of Sinshan Creek, published in *Always Coming Home* (1985).

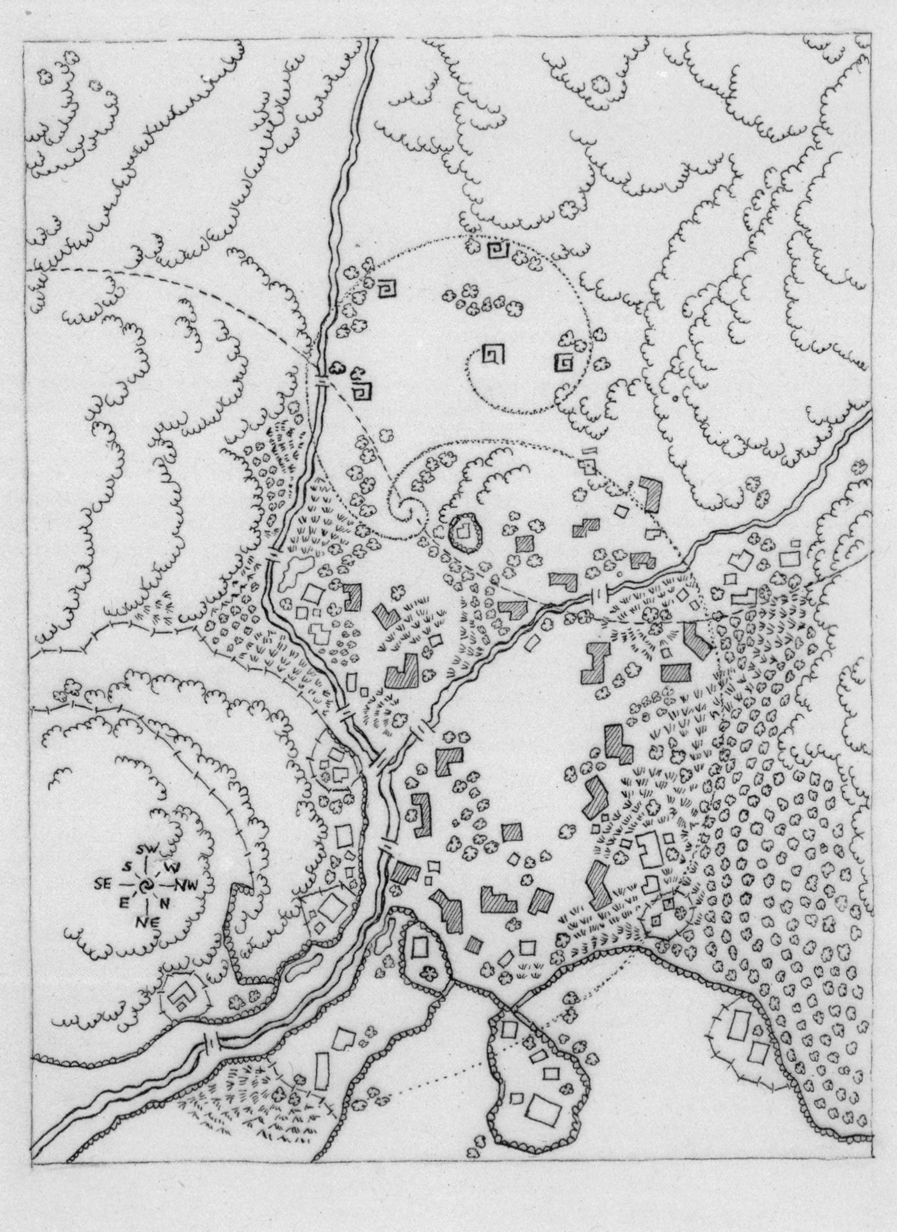

The Town of Sinshan, published in *Always Coming Home* (1985).

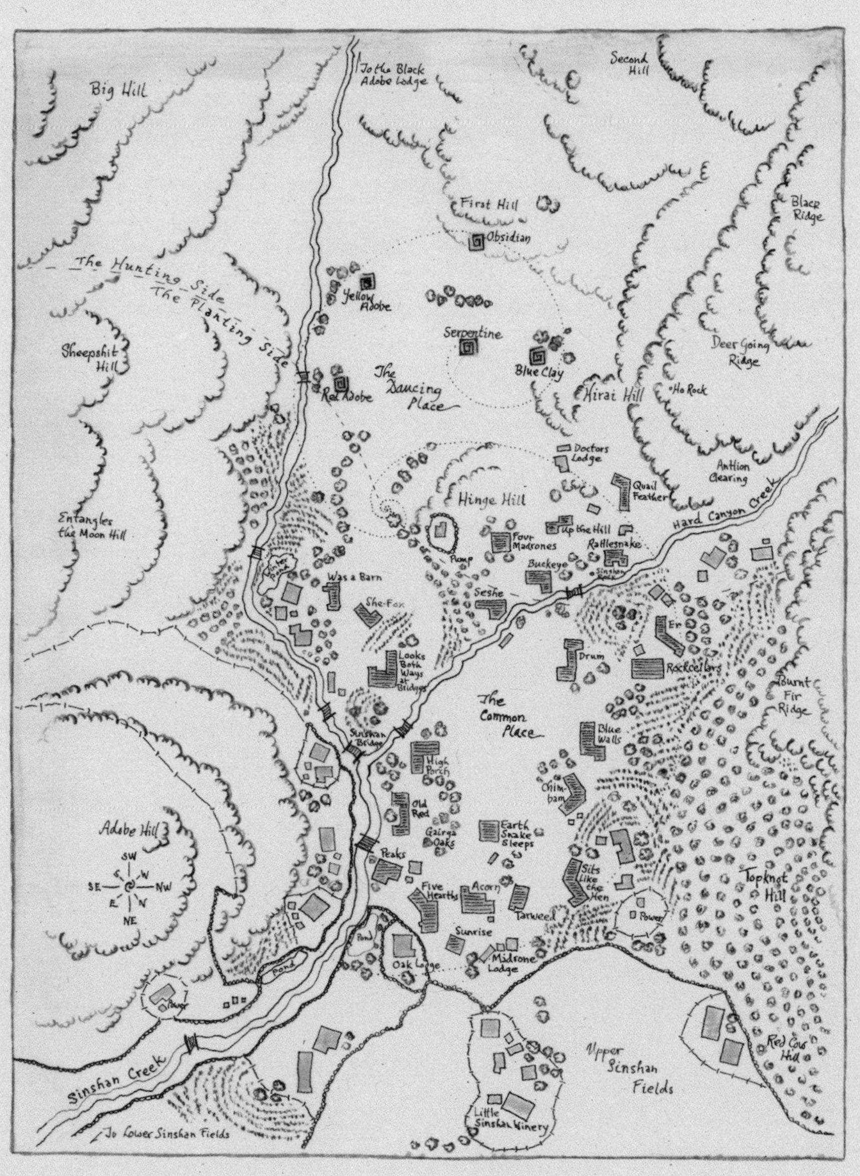

The Town of Sinshan, unpublished,
for *Always Coming Home* (1985)

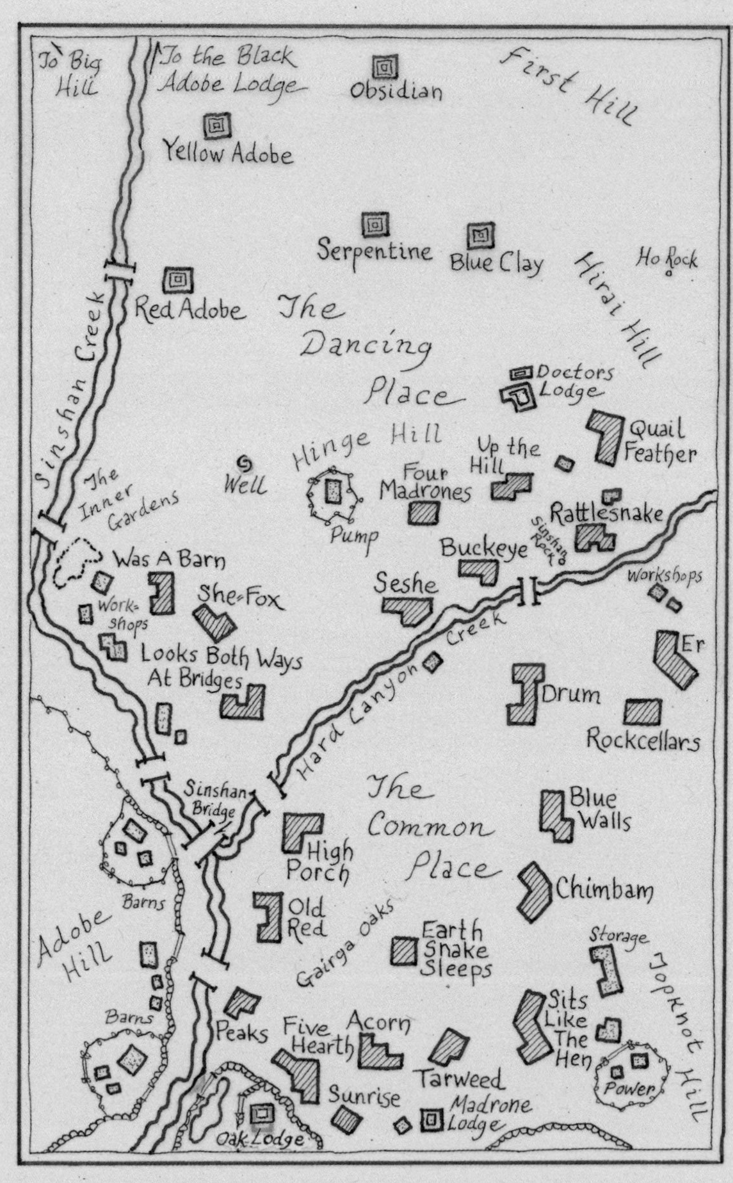

The Names of the Houses of Sinshan, published in *Always Coming Home* (1985).

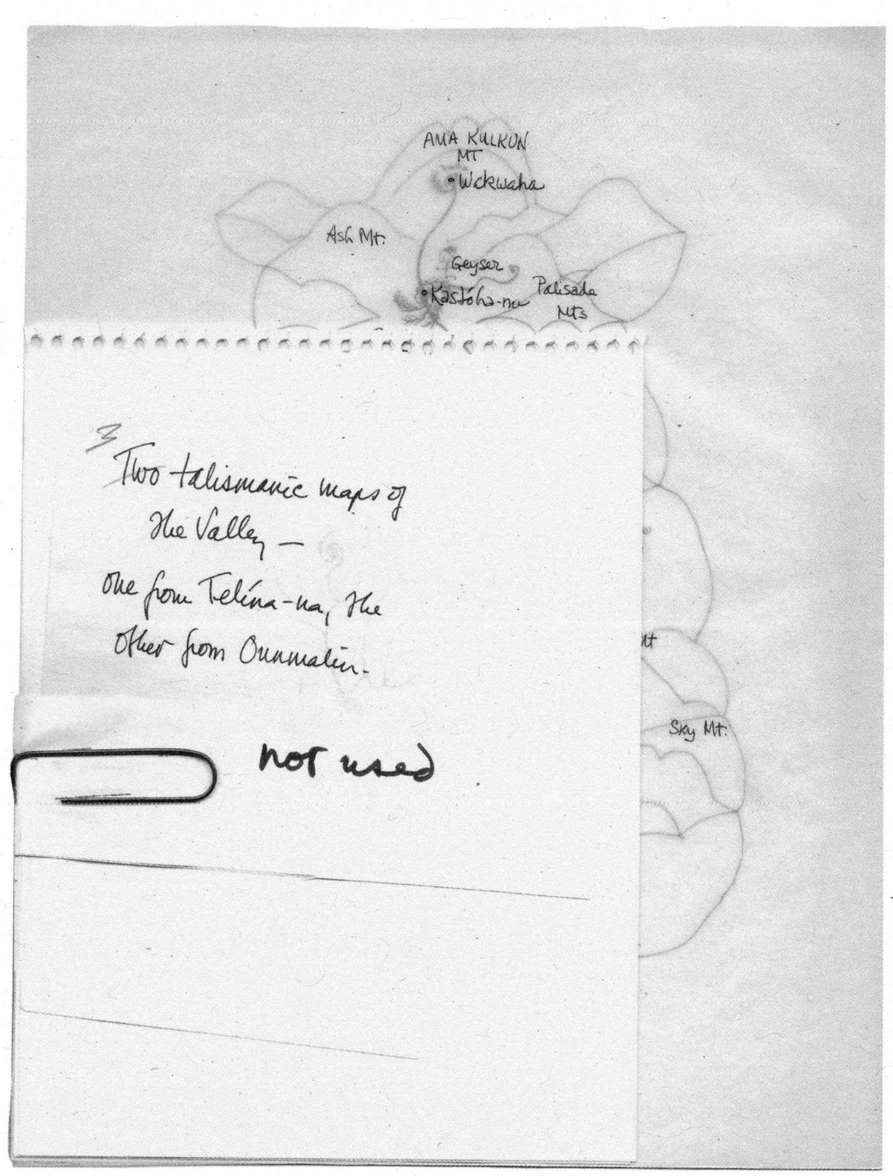

Cover note for three talismanic maps of the Valley, unpublished, for *Always Coming Home* (1985)

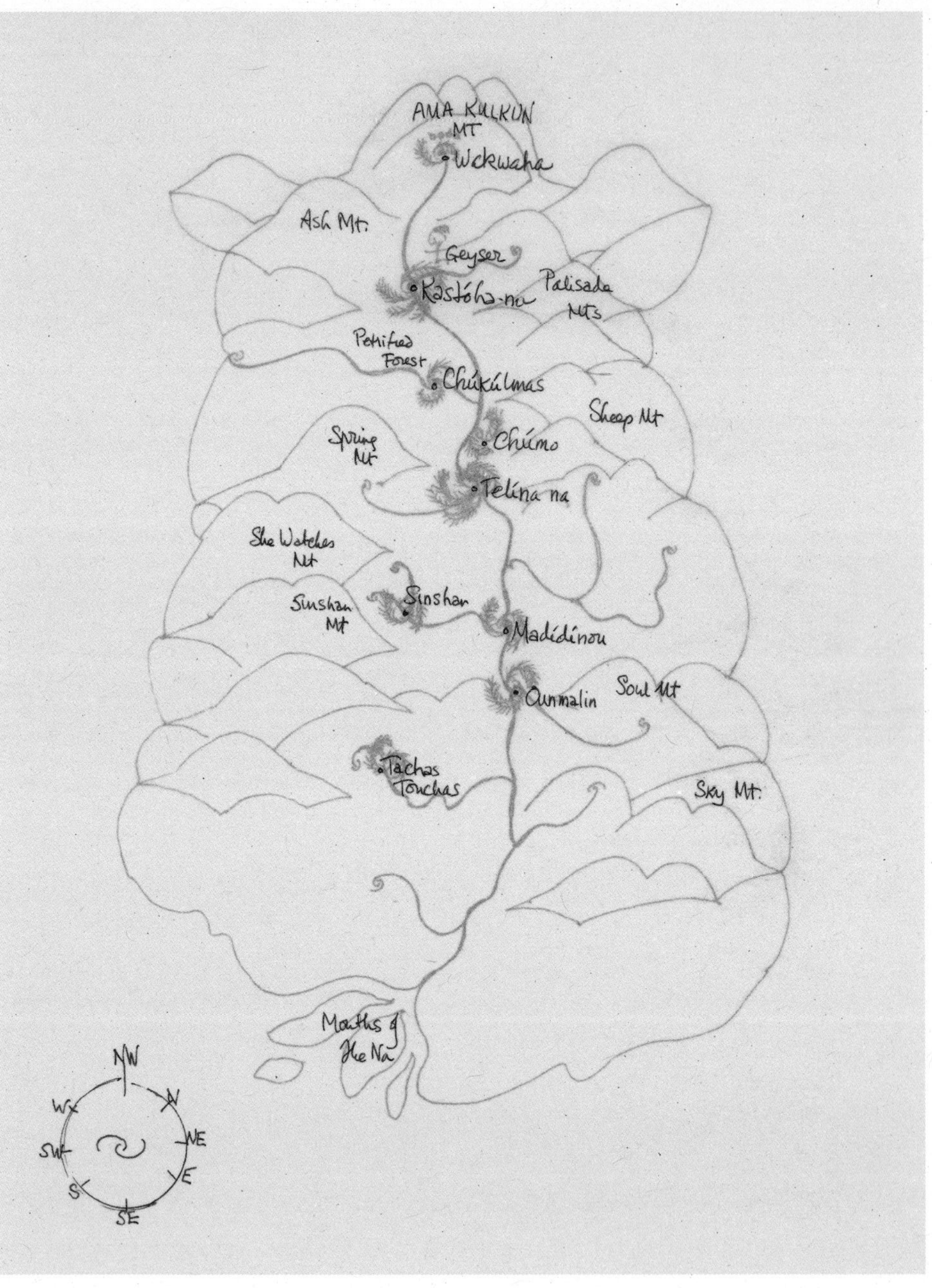

Talismanic map of the Valley, unpublished, for *Always Coming Home* (1985).

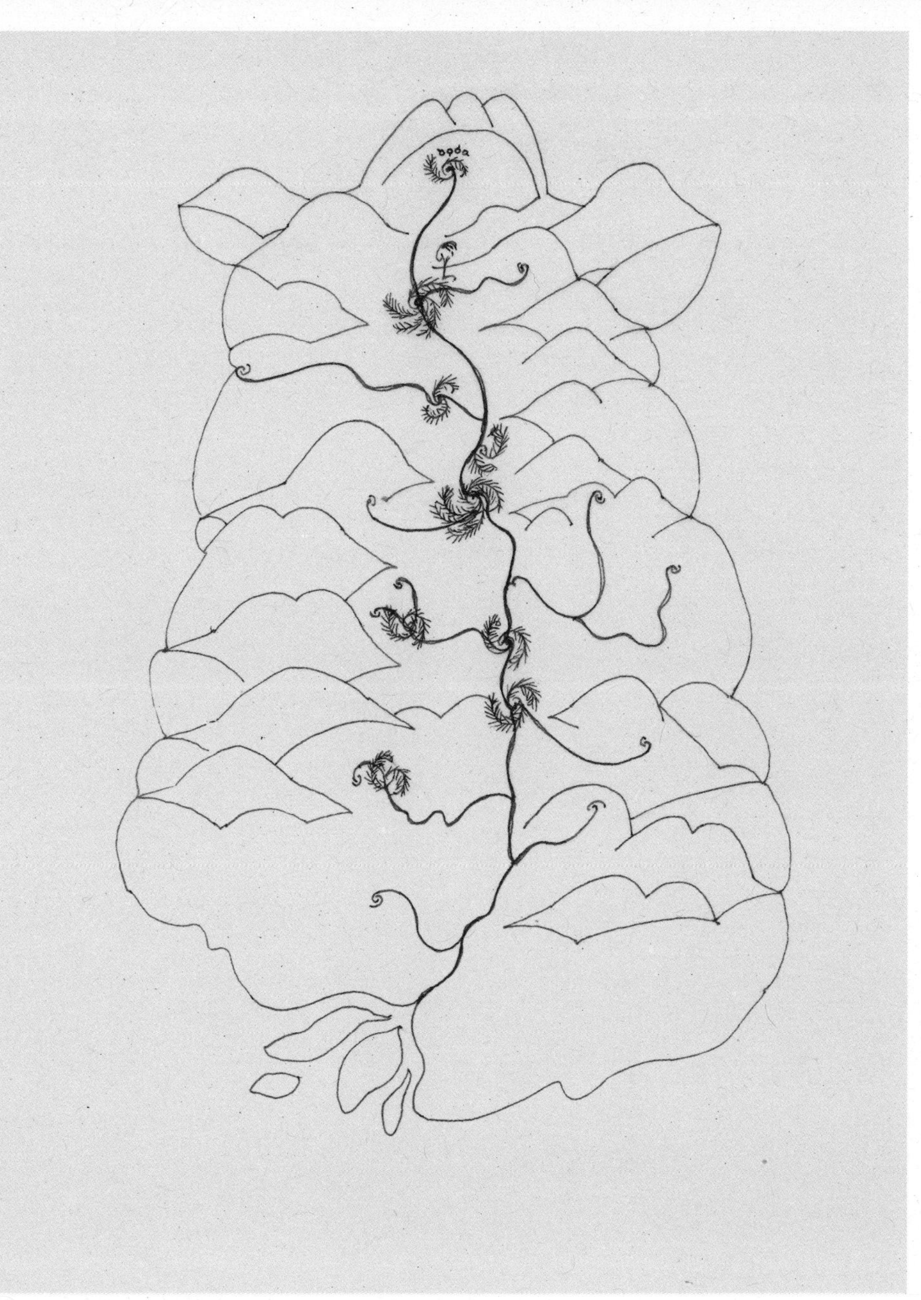

Talismanic map of the Valley, unpublished, for *Always Coming Home* (1985).

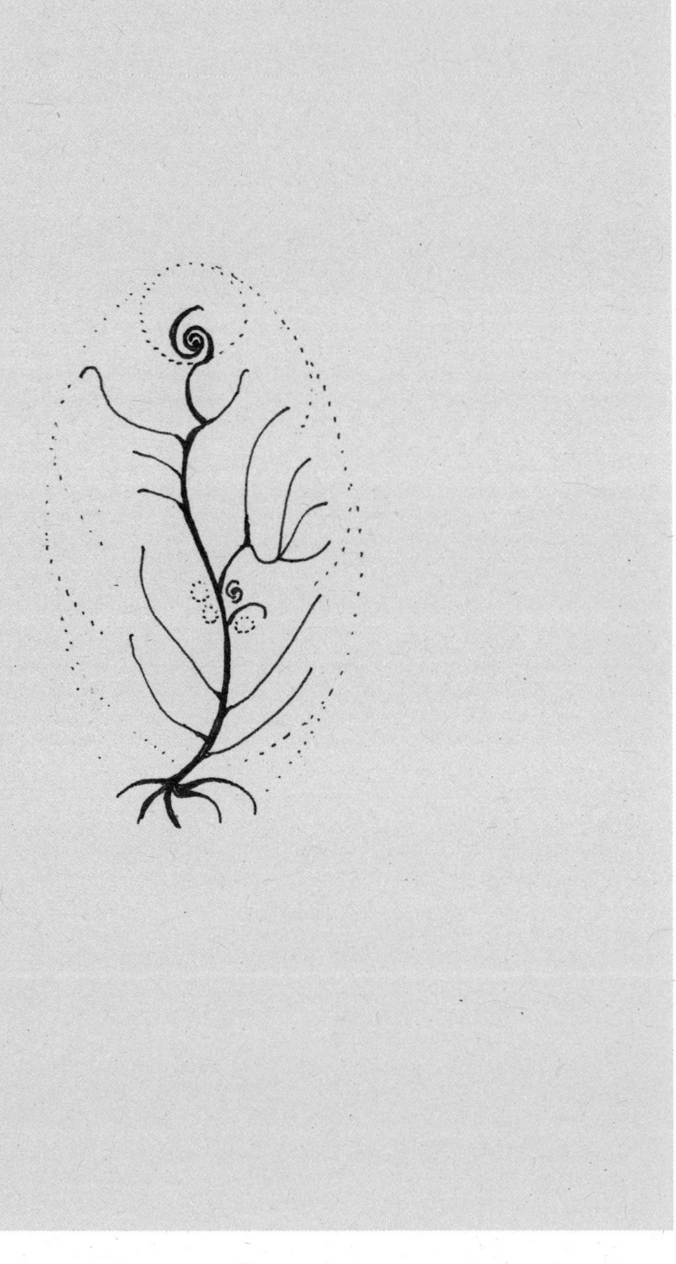

Talismanic map of the Valley, unpublished, for *Always Coming Home* (1985).

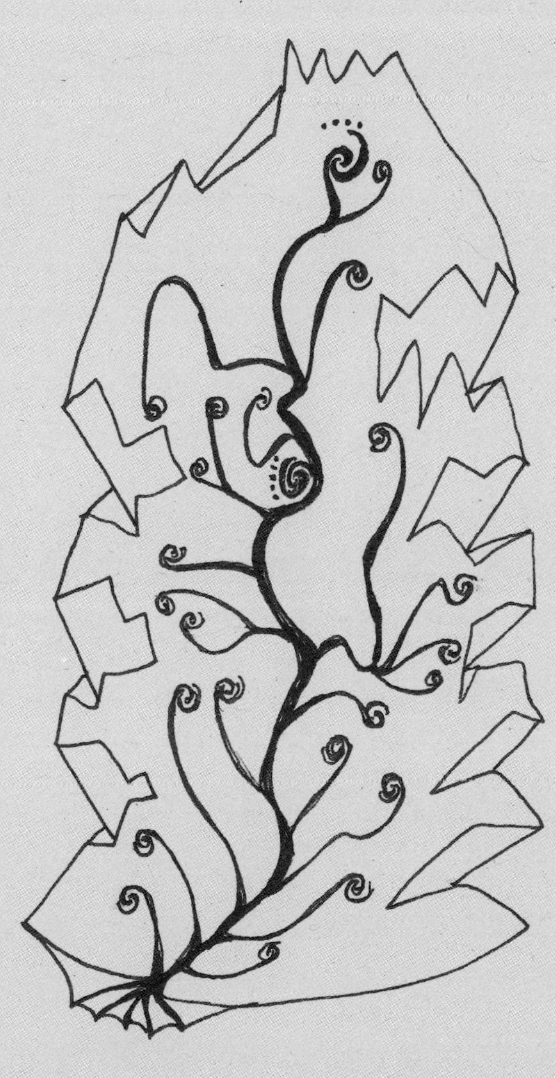

Talismanic map of the Valley, unpublished,
for *Always Coming Home* (1985).

Federico Campagna

Seasons

The burnt yellow of the cereal fields around Prizzi, my father's village in the Sicilian inland, was at its peak. Under the limestone cliffs, resplendent in the sun, the black mark of the plough was eating away at the slopes and valleys. On the high valley at the foot of the mountain, the cluster of peasant cottages was abuzz with a special commotion. A ceaseless chitchat poured through the curtains onto the clearing with the tractors and manure, breaking the calm of a late August morning. Just a few weeks ago, the emigrants had returned from Germany. Now they were cramming the trunks of their cars with boxes of tomato passata, cans of oil, bundles of oregano. Whenever I chased a mis-kicked ball out of the stone arch of our house, I would see another group of elderly relatives lined along the potholed street. The emigrants did not tire of kissing and embracing them, one by one. The father entered the car, then the kids and lastly the mother. They waved their hands out of the windows, as if to disperse something invisible into the air. Every morning, one of those vessels with foreign license plates and dashboards lined in synthetic fur started its engine to set sail. The relatives stood on the pavement until the car had disappeared around the bend of the highway. Then the women returned home, and the men walked slowly to tend to the cows. Another year would pass; who knew who would be missing at the next reunion.

It was during those late Augusts of my childhood that I first realised how the time of migrants differs from that marked on calendars. For a migrant, time unfolds along two parallel lines: the suspended instant of their lost homeland and the rhythm of work in a distant land. To neither time are they completely present, in neither place are they truly at home. The border between these dimensions opens on specific dates, sad celebrations without a name. Even today, these thresholds mark my own time; as if, at the end of every August, I still had to get in the car with my family, take the road to the port and return up North, to Milan, where my own parents had migrated.

But to those who have never migrated, all this remains hidden – not only the seams between nameless seasons, but also other, mysterious distortions of reality. They might ignore, for example, that every land exists in more than one dimension. In one of them, it is made up of buildings, trees, soil and water; it can be photographed by satellites, it can be reached by car or plane. It is open to the return of those who wandered away, but only temporarily and never fully. In its second dimension, however, the same land does not correspond to any geographical location. While invisible to everyone else, it is always at hand for those who once called it home – they need only search within their memories, fantasies and dislocated hopes. If both these dimensions are real, it is only the latter that the migrant experiences as their reality.

From their distant lives, as strangers in a foreign land, migrants do not let a day pass without returning to their imagined homeland. Without formal training in metaphysics, they know how to unlock the doors between the different strata of reality, travelling distances that would seem insurmountable to others. The Sicilian summers of my childhood, and the seasons my parents and I had to spend in Milan for work and study, fostered in me an early interest in the imaginary aspect of world-building. I knew by experience that the intuition of migrants – like the gaze with which only a lover can see the unfathomable depths of their beloved – reveals an authentic feature of reality. How little is within the grasp of maps, satellites and travel agencies! Infinite expanses stretch out beyond the material and measurable aspects of existence, perceptible only through the imagination and nonetheless entirely real.

Such an awareness often dawns in the wake of a profound loss, whether of one's homeland or a loved one. Suddenly one realises, with a clarity that is no longer merely conceptual, that the material disappearance of an object does not imply its total annihilation. Even though it has become invisible and undetectable even to machines, some of its parts have remained intact. Materiality is only one of the dimensions through which reality reveals itself and our ability to measure it with apparent precision has given us an exaggerated sense of its importance. The existence of an object – any object, be it a person, a land, or the whole world – includes all the aspects that we can perceive through our imagination, stretching even beyond the field of the imaginable. The persistence of an object in our mind after it has materially disappeared – and the life that it continues to lead within our imagination, engaged in an endless series of metamorphoses – reveal glimpses of its existence in dimensions that lie outside the realm governed by space and time. Indeed, it already existed in those dimensions while it was still materially visible, but its true extent remained obfuscated until loss finally unveiled it. Like the organs of physical perception, the imagination also discloses something authentic about the infinite wealth of reality.

What might sound like a fantasy born out of grief is in fact a philosophical intuition shared by thinkers from antiquity to the present age. Reality, considered in itself and as a whole, is a *chaos* so deep and immense that it exceeds any possibility of being understood or experienced. Even something as small as a pebble, if we consider it to the full extent of its existence, becomes a mystery beyond comprehension. We can detect only a fragment of this *chaos*, as it is filtered by our perceptive apparatus and cognitive limits. Through our imagination, based on our personal inclinations and on the cosmological assumptions of our society, we mould this remaining piece into one of the infinite forms that reality can take. This activity of the imagination provides us with a *cosmos*, a 'world', a place where we can develop those structures of sense that shelter us from the trauma of having been thrown, unprepared, into a mortal life. Then, spurred by the force of habit and by a desire for comfort, we become progressively convinced that the world we have constructed is an accurate picture of 'nature', and that reality coincides with the metaphysical consensus of a particular society at a certain moment in human history. We tend to forget the imaginary essence of the 'world' that we see around ourselves and we start drawing hard distinctions between what we deem as 'truly existing' and what we set aside as 'mere fantasy'.

Over the years, this philosophical enquiry merged with a personal sense of longing for my own fantasy of a lost Mediterranean homeland, leading me to undertake extensive research into the many ways in which, over the millennia, the people of the Mediterranean have filtered and reinvented their experience of reality. Towards them, who lived and died in societies rather different from my own, I felt more familiarity than distance. Studying the remnants of their literature and artefacts, I recognised how multitudes of common people – not counting the philosophers and theologians, who specialise in these sorts of speculations – lived suspended between 'here' and 'there': the time and space imagined by their society, where they could be disciplined and punished; and another plane, where their surroundings were the product of their own imagination. This is not a unique feature of the Mediterranean. But in the Mediterranean, this imaginary practice has developed a range of characteristics that renders it worthy of special attention.

The Mediterranean has known moments of astonishing splendour, such as the civilisations of the ancient Egyptians, Greeks and Romans, of the Arabs and the Ottomans, whose impact on global history and culture cannot be overestimated. Each of these peaks, however, was followed by an apocalyptic catastrophe. Every great Mediterranean civilisation eventually crumbled and collapsed, dragging the people who assumed its cultural values as their own through something that could justly be described as the 'end of the world'. The fall of a civilisation does not only consist in the fraying of its social fabric, together with its political, economic and technological infrastructures, but also in the disintegration of its common sense of the nature of the world, which used to stand as the imaginary foundation of a meaningful life. When these fundamental values falter, and then eventually fall, *chaos* begins to seep through the cracks of *cosmos*.

The peoples of the Mediterranean had to face a long series of such traumatising events, accompanied by material disasters like wars, famines and plagues. In response to these cyclical apocalypses, they devised a range of radical strategies of survival. Whenever historical upheavals laid waste to their material and immaterial world, many decided to migrate in search of an elsewhere that would allow their life to flourish once more. They moved through space, like the economic migrants of which my family and I are also examples, but most importantly, they also moved beyond space and time, outside the confines of History. Instead of clinging to the values of a vanishing world or embracing those of the new rising powers, they dared to migrate to the ground zero of the imagination, where ideas and values can be extracted anew from the infinite virtuality of the possible.

These deserters from History had to face the hostility both of those who remained attached to the old world and of those heralding the triumph of a new order. Their quest to invent a different reality was often a solitary adventure, and even when they managed to congregate in groups, most of their sailings ended in shipwreck. History showed little mercy to communities such as the last Pagans of antiquity, the Manicheans, or the mystic Jews of the Italian Renaissance. They were systematically ground to dust and their visions failed to prevail as a new common sense about the nature of the world. But despite their defeat, their invention of new *cosmoi* endured as a testament to how a person's vision of the world can be untangled from dominant social forces, and the *chaos* of reality can be reclothed within narratives that arise from an individual's suffering and desire for life.

To the people who inhabited the creations of the Mediterranean imagination as their own world, their power resided less in the impeccability of their conceptual structure than in the charm of their narrative. Even the most sophisticated theory remains sterile if it lacks the immersive quality of literature. Unless it stands as a story that can be experienced from within, like a game of role play or a theatre piece, it fails to provide a convincing illusion of meaning and thus it is not accepted as a viable human 'world'.

Excerpted from *Otherworlds: Mediterranean Lessons On Escaping History* (2025).

Nisha Ramayya

this place is a message

where have you been, walking
in the present horror, I heard your steps
and knew you unduly, not knowing the grammar
of your telling. subvert the perversions
of language, its lethal currents –
categories that kill, stock phrases that legitimise
decimation.
        some words are pebbles, some sentences
stones, some books mountains. poetry is a promiscuous
heap. I close my eyes to your whereabouts,
risking palms and soles on the increscence of your answers
clambering silvery thorns towards something, somewhere –
us, here. these stones, their messages, how dissonant
        they'll sound
to the gorge walkers, grasping in dreams
with bleeding hands, ears turned to brokenness
indiscrete at the bottom, our tears.
cairns mark the headwaters, glancing
moots between a way that was and a way that clowns
glacial nevers and vaporous always
unsettling homewards, word rivering returns

Legend

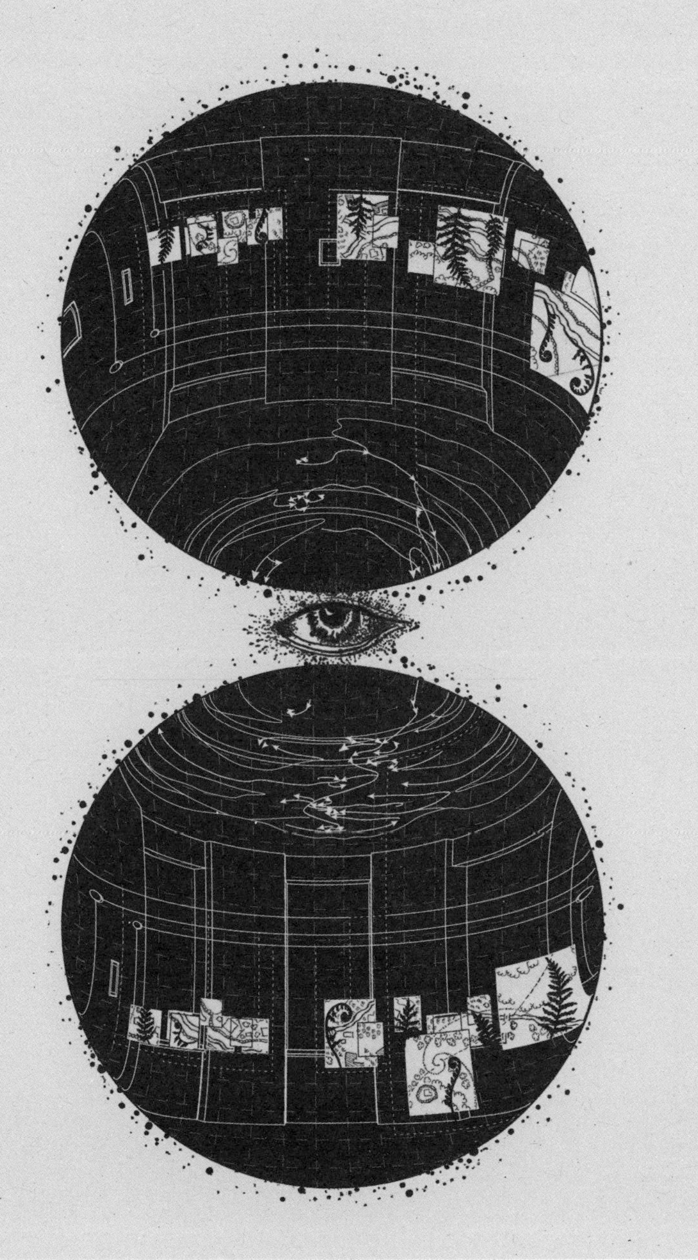

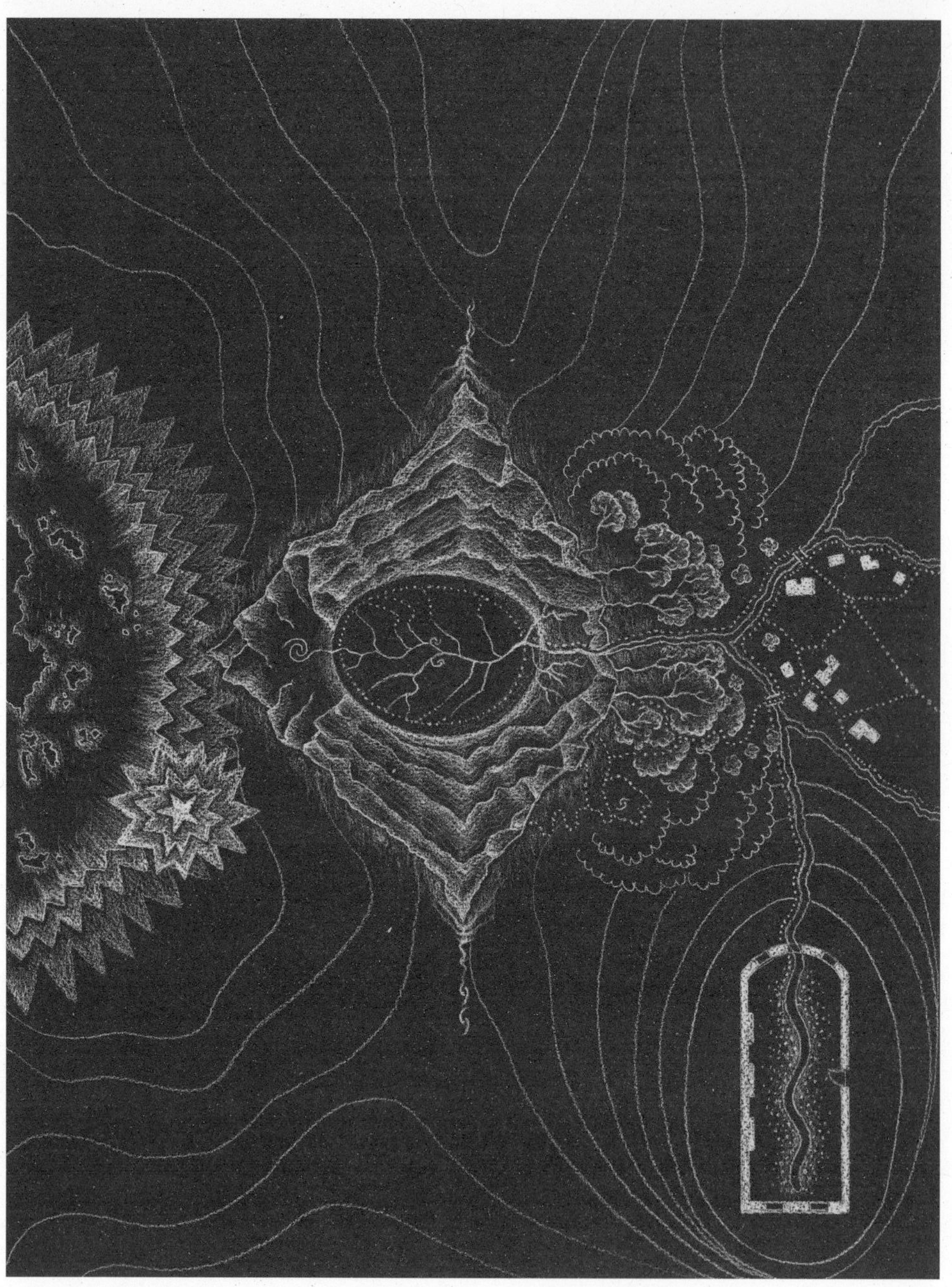

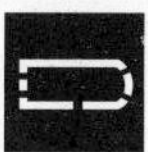

At the beginning of the universe, there was a girl who was the youngest daughter of Earth and Sky. One day, the goddess was bored and she fell asleep. In her dream, she went to consult the oracle book in the seed library that contained all the seeds in the world. Opening the book, she found rows and rows of seeds. When the girl woke up, a stream of seeds poured from her forehead.

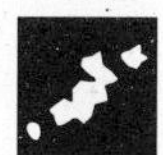

An archipelago emerged where the seeds fell into the vast blue, each island a world within a world. Each island was slung around a mountain, where time turned into space.

Each mountain was contained in a pebble that the goddess carried in her pocket, taking every mountain to form a pile of pebbles: an impossible mountain floating in the sky, reaching downwards and upwards.

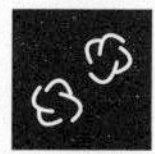

At the foothills of the mountain, the forest floated up from the darkness. Here were the shadows that rose up to make themselves known; here were the forces that appeared to be opposites but in fact held the other, like a dragon eating its own tail.

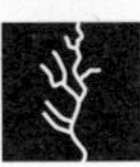

The goddess spent her summers in the valley, roaming its land along the river. She learned to write and to draw, recreating the place in deep blues extracted from the valley soil.

To carry the memory of the valley of the island, she made a talisman. From it flowed a river of words, from which flowed stories about journeys across galaxies.

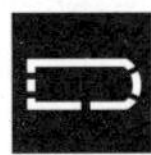

The river ran by the house, which contained the uncontainable – connection, spiral and change. In the night, the house was the universe, where the girl dreamed of a world of winter, houses of blue adobe, a labyrinth in complete darkness and a forest of dreams. In the day, the goddess and her friends let sunlight fall through leaves to make blueprints, and hung these plans and maps of the worlds of their imagination around her father's library that contained all the seeds in the world.

Bhanu Kapil

The Clearing

1.

Is it true that we choose our families? That we drop from a silver cloud into the map, scraping our bare arms and legs on the branches of the fir tree outside the house with the ochre roof? And if that's true, then does our mother unhook us from a bough, wrap us in a flour sack and tuck us in a drawer? Come morning, she checks. To see. If.

Yes, you're still alive. But if they find you? If they open the drawer with a rough gesture? If they choose that day, that hour, to conduct their search? If they enter without knocking? If they break down the door? If the neighbour, glassy-eyed, half-asleep, pushes back their curtains as you fall from the sky? Frankie! Frankie, get in here right now. And if Frankie, her partner, that well-known bag of nerves, is the one who makes the call? Sorry, darling, but if we don't. They might. We can't.

Take the risk? And so it was that my mother slipped me into a tote. Off to the market. If glimpsed. In her hand, crumpled, a list. Flowers, bread, milk. If stopped. With a sigh, that genius, my mother, paused in the drive-way, hand on the brake. There's something about the warmth of a car on a sunny day with brisk wind. It's like a hug. Should she crack a window? Turn on the radio? You never know. I was quiet, immobile. Not a peep. A good baby. Good baby. Easy now.

A city, far from sea, is an inland port. The border is not a line. Descend. To a border. Only to hover there forever. We drove all day. Away from the border then further in. At dusk, we slipped over a hill and there it was. A smudge on the horizon. A ridge, and when we reached it. A forest. Vertical. Vibrating so hard it had no colour. But it was green. It had to be green. You flexed then contracted your brown limbs. Slipping the bottle from my bag, I massaged you with almond oil. Warm from the car. From the journey. As light rain fell. On the roof.

2.

The forest moves in an anticlockwise fashion, then clockwise again. Imagine a plush material distended by a careless hand. The flank of a leopard pressed flat against tall grass. Spikes of gelatine yellow where a leaf snapped off. Cuckoo-spit bubbling on the stem. Smudge of sun through the violet clouds. To recall the second day is a memory beyond seasons. I knew I had to hide you. I knew I had to hide myself. The car?

She drove it into the thick part. We walked from there. A twig snapped. Glow-worms swarmed. A spiral has no augur. My mother kicked her sneakers off. To stand on the prickles of the earth. How else to experience the telluric drag of the clearing's force? I was in her arms. Was this the way? Your only job is to perish in deep love, said my mother, repeating the lines of a song she sang in her own mother's lap. Or had her mother sung to her?

Doesn't matter if your beloved doesn't give two hoots to your love.

3.

In a clearing is a shallow bowl. Imagine a ceramic bowl, mud-grey on the outside. But on the inside is an azure glaze. It gives you a feeling of courage just to see it, a new colour that produces its own light. And at the centre of the bowl, pooled there, is a large, intact drop of water. You would think it is a jewel. You would think it was made by someone with a musical touch, dangling and drooping their head over fine work. Just then, it pops. The bottom of the bowl is wet. Leaning in, you observe a grille. The water dribbles through. Imagine a butterfly or moth with red bands on its light gold wings. The red has the intensity of a thousand berries. Here it is. The butterfly. Alighting. To slurp. Proboscis slipping. Through a tiny hole. Just as many flowers have evolved to nourish insects rather than animals, this bowl retains its gold.

Who put it there?

4.

You can do this. You are not a fake lover. If you don't perish in love, it brings you fame. Come on. If you don't perish in love, you'll grieve a lot. Don't lose your efforts to love. And only love. It brings you fame. If you spend your life. Hovering around the light. Lovers don't die. Their love remains, sang my mother. Yes, you can do this, I said to my mother without words. The vibration of my mother's words entered my body through her back ribs. Taut against her back in the cotton sling, I felt no pain.

The lovers don't lie. Their love remains. Go on. Don't worry about the threats. This world gives you. Go on. Flow. In the ocean of love, sang my mother. Your job is to love and perish. Crazy lover. Go on loving forever.

The night made friends with us. Tiny lamps hovered above the branches; fluorescent snakes slipped before us on the dark path.

Imagine that in the middle of our little star is a triangular cave where a grizzly bear lives. If you open the door of his cave, the bear starts to eat the flowers that grow and curl above the threshold and on the ground. The flowers blossom all year round, sustaining the mother bear with his great red heart.

Bobbing on my mother's back, swaddled, was I writing? I, who had never seen a bear, had not yet reached. The story of the star. Or was this the stage before writing?

Your job is to love and perish.

Almost there.

5.

One day, your neighbour knocks on your door. That early warning saves your family. Glancing back at your home before you close the door for the last time, you see the bowl on the sideboard. It's fragile, but you grab it, wrapping it in your coat. You make it as far as the station, or perhaps the street, before you're stopped. Your neighbour has betrayed you. Your life as a family has come to an end, you understand, as the van screeches to a halt.

Delicate artefacts are set down on the asphalt, thrice wrapped. They change hands, then once again. A century passes. Another. Now here it is, the delicate artefact.

Here. There.

Here.

6.

Is it true that we become a family in the same way that a figurative line gradually disappears? My memories of this time in the forest were the basis of my future art, the underworld writing that thrashed my fate, just as the society my mother survived gave her everything she needed to flee it. Her bright fear coupled with a faint memory of her own mother's mother, the long beard and grey braids of a grandmother ape. They visited her once, in a clearing. In a clearing? There's coolness here, a brightness and coolness, deep in the forest, that's familiar to her. More familiar than the trees, which are languid at this hour. They are, after all, dependents of the sun. Here, in the roots of a cedar tangled with a secondary vine of a little white rose, are two eggs in a nest. It took enormous strength to lay those, says my mother, cracking one into her mouth. I lick the yolk. From her fingertip. A conference of owlish faces. All around. Peeking out. As we bobbed along. She was mine. I was hers. How did she know?

Many years later, when I saw my face in a mirror for the first time, the forest appeared in the mercury, the metal layer behind the glass. Faint green, light pink, the forest was present in the air around my body, implanted there on the walk with my mother.

It was not a human face.

7.

When I was a child and when my mother. Was my mother. We foraged in the nearby scrub. Our society had not averted the catastrophe foretold in even the most intimate relationships or private contexts. Even the doctors had fled, taking their medicines with them. When my stomach was unsettled, my mother nourished me with a cloudy tonic made from three berries, gathered then dried, a churan or powder she added to water then stirred with a knife. Returning with her basket from the forest on those foraging days, she nodded to our neighbours, shrugging and smiling as she held up the fruit. Well-known as a local healer, nobody thought twice when she left for stretches, hours, on soft afternoons, or at dusk on the days a full moon fell. Nobody called the hotline. Nobody saw her, really, in her long cotton dress printed with Autumn leaves. At tree-line, I stepped into the fold of her skirt as she in turn, my mother, stepped into forest thought.

Slipping off her sandals, she stood in her socks upon the ground until she felt it.

The twitch.

If a spiral has arms. If each arm is a path. If we buried the shards at intervals. Meteorites, rubies, quartz. And if, as the moon rose, the path beneath the path began to glow.

Whether midnight or noon. Whether the sky was clear or filled with smoke.

And on moonless nights?

Kneeling down, she unbuckled my shoes.

So you can feel it too, said my mother.

How else would I have known?

8.

Just past the stand of bamboo is a low wooden platform. A bowl on the ground, the butterfly host. Are we here?

The first time I saw her, still as still at the edge of the clearing, I thought she was a dolmen, a standing stone. A face so unlike the faces of. Others. Flinching, I clung to my mother's leg. To see a face we'd been taught. To watch for. To stop. To scream when we. Met. But with a sob, my mother ran towards her. I fell back onto the soft grass as the stone trembled. The face was real: whiskers, beard, nose running with snot. Eyes a-glint. Thick brown fur to the wrist. Barking with joy, she pulled my mother to her chest.

Then me.

9.

Describe a clearing in the forest where a Monkey-mother meditates, spinning and buzzing all around. At the edge of the clearing, a hunter raises his bow then lets it drop, feeling a tingling at the back of his own head. Soon, he's spinning too, right into the place where the Monkey-mother is. Guru-ji, says the hunter, soon we shall both destroy the demons together.

Yes, said the Monkey-mother, an eternal presence who could eat fire, who lived beyond the end of stories only to reappear in another book.

10.

When I was a baby. When we fled. When it was time to go. When I fell from the sky. When there were no ancestors. When there were no offspring. No citizen or non-citizen with human, animal and alien mixtures coursing through their forms. Allowed to live. Persist. Pair off. Thrive. When my own mother shaved her face and arms every day. And when she saw me, caught on the branch. When she saw the fur. When she saw my face. She knew. What to do.

11.

Sometimes our ancestors are waiting for us, just ahead. Here, in the clearing, Monkey-mother presses flower petals to our faces, sticking them down with the tip of her tongue. She takes me from my mother's arms and hugs me close. I've been waiting for you, she says.

Is it true that there's a life beyond surveillance, corrosion, the turn to subjective rule? Is it true that what's coming next is a cull?

This is the story of my babyhood. To tell you what happens next, to answer these questions, I would have to draw you another map. I would have to crush jewels. I would have to build a spiral extending from my home to the perimeter of the place you are living in now. I would have to clear a space. I would have to make a tea and bring it to the one who is still there, ripening, sucking water from the dark green leaves. I would have to comb her beard and oil it down.

You don't need a map.

Drape a towel over your shoulder, and if anyone stops you. Point to the sea. Tell them it's hot. See you later. I'm off.

For a swim.

That way, nobody will notice.

When you take off your shoes.

To stand on the bright green grass.

An Interview with Daniel Heath Justice

Cartographic Kinscapes

So Mayer (SM), Daniel Heath Justice (DHJ)

SM: Why make maps for fantasy novels? I'm intrigued by your take on this as a fantasy novelist, scholar and teacher of creative writing.

DHJ: When I use world-building exercises in teaching science fiction and fantasy, I never mandate a map. If students choose to develop one, we'd have a conversation, because a map is never just a map, it's always an ideological argument. I'd ask: what is the geography that you are highlighting? Who are the people who live here? Who are the people who are excluded from this map? How do you attend to people who aren't constrained by settlements in this particular way?

SM: The way Le Guin talks about it in the introduction to *The Birthday of the World and Other Stories* is that she 'did not plan these worlds and people [but] found them, gradually, piecemeal, while writing stories', and got to know them deeper and deeper. Does that resonate with your process of drawing the maps for your Indigenous fantasy trilogy *The Way of Thorn and Thunder: The Kynship Chronicles*?

DHJ: Returning again and again to the familiar creates a deeper bond. It's intimacy. The map in *Kynship Chronicles* was about giving texture to a world that I was travelling in. It wasn't about defining the space; it was a way for me to better understand its relationships, and relationships across time and space.

Practically, I wanted to understand how distant particular communities are from one another, but also what their relationships are to one another. If you're living downriver, what happens upriver is going to impact you down below. What are the trade routes, what are the kinship exchange routes? What are the places where people are potentially going to come into conflict with one another? What are the places of potential gathering and shared purpose? So it was never a question of how we *define* a place, as much as how we understand that place through its relationships.

SM: How was that realised in the flat, two-dimensional plan, given that the maps we see in fantasy novels mostly adhere to Eurocolonial cartographic conventions?

DHJ: *The Kynship Chronicles* is a removal story, though one set in a secondary world. Because it's connected to the idea of Cherokee removal, I never really saw the maps outside of the effort of people to hold on to their land. Even though there are these conventions, and there are ways in which these maps very much reflect Eurocolonial acquisition, they also capture something about imperilled belonging. The maps didn't exist outside of that threat of dispossession.

A lot of fantasy maps are about creating a stage for conflict or adventure and exploration. In my book, the Folk didn't need to explore. They already know this land and the relationships that are part of it. They're just trying to hold on. The Everland inset map, showing the Folk's remaining territory (p 102), is much, much more detailed with more communities, more relationships articulated. The larger map of the Melded World (p 103) is pretty bland and vague. The Everland is a textured space, because that's where the relationships are. When I was mapping where the Kyn and Tetawi and other Folk lived, it was to understand why they were holding on so tightly and what geopolitical pressures they were under. I can't think of a way in which the map would have been about defining the land outside of relationships.

SM: The compass rose made of spears and corn tassels alerts the reader to that, in that it appears on the Everland map, but not on the Melded World map. Compass roses were significant to Le Guin: as well as naming one of her short story collections *The Compass Rose*, she often drew elaborate compass roses on her maps. And they don't always have north as their orientation point, they're often tilted on an axis.

DHJ: If I were to redraw my maps today, I wouldn't have north on there. That came from talking with Elder Larry Grant from the Musqueam Nation a number of years ago, who pointed out that in Musqueam tradition, the cardinal directions don't really exist. The two directions that mattered were *upriver* and *downriver*, because those are the directions that languages and relations flow. That broke my head open a little, realising, 'Oh, of course!' For us, back in our old territories, it was the mountains: our towns were linguistically and even culturally distinguished by where you were in the mountains and valleys of the Great Smoky Mountains. There's the Overhill, Valley, Middle, and Lower Towns. At one point, we had three different dialects of Cherokee, which were geographically distinct depending on where you were in the mountains. In the novel I'm working on now, the mountain is what matters. The *mountain* is the cardinal point.

SM: In some ways, having a map at the beginning of a book of fiction already throws off some Eurocolonial conventions of reading. It's not linear and unidirectional, because you might be flipping to the front, or might even draw your own. In science fiction and fantasy in particular, it also challenges readers' assumptions about cartography as producing an objective document of the known or 'real' world.

DHJ: It anchors you in the otherwise. It automatically says, 'This is a foreign country. This is a place that you are new to. Even if it's ostensibly our world, it's our world askew.' It signals to you that, whatever your expectations are, you can't rely on them. It's productively destabilising: for those of us who are steeped in the conventions of the genre, that's where we want to be. People who are new to it can be quite disoriented, but that's part of the point.

I encountered this first in reading *The Wonderful Wizard of Oz*. I think I had read *The Hobbit* before I read the Oz books, but it was the Oz maps that surprised me, because over time the map changes, and it changes really significantly. The first map in *The Wonderful Wizard of Oz* is very different from the one that follows with the other books. I eventually found a book of Oz ephemera, and it was so fascinating to me that you could have so many different maps of the same place. I realised that, as the books proceeded, the map was filled in more. I got the idea that the story itself populates the land, and that affects the map as well, and that made me want to make my own.

So I created my own little Oz, and I started to do the same with Tolkien. Then I discovered D&D (*Dungeons & Dragons*), which encourages you to make your own world with all these familiar tropes, figures and people. You get to decide where the mountains are. You get to decide where the towns are. It's a reminder that there are other ways of being, imagining and existing. Even if it's ostensibly of our world, the map is always going to be a little bit off.

There are other ways of mapping, too. I think a lot about Mississippian cosmology, this idea that we're part of the three-tiered world. It's a conceptual map: the Upper World, the Below World, and this Middle World that we exist on, so you get into much more abstract ideas of where we are in relation to other beings in the cosmos. I love that the more abstract the map, the more it makes you think about your place and your role in these relationships.

The Mayan codices that were persecuted and destroyed by the Spanish: they're book-formed in ways that are now familiar, but they're also wildly distinctive. The Mayan cosmological map as seen in the codices is also a kind of relational or genealogical chart of the gods, and genealogy is itself a kind of map through space and time. Those codices unfold like an accordion, and the world unfolds. They were intended to be spoken, to be an extension of human voice and body. They don't hold knowledge without the People.

SM: Both those ideas – genealogy being a kind of map, and documents not holding knowledge without the People – feel very much connected to your current scholarly research on allotment, in the collection you co-edited with Jean M O'Brien, *Allotment Stories: Indigenous Land Relations Under Settler Siege*.

DHJ: For Cherokees in what's currently called Oklahoma, mapping has been inextricably connected with dispossession. It's now also very much part of reconnection and resurgence: those same maps that were used in part to strip us of our relations to land are helping us to restore relations not just to land, but to kin.

The allotment maps were created by the Dawes Commission, a government agency tasked with breaking up and individualising our collective lands, but they reflect so much of Cherokee efforts to maintain sovereignty and kinship: if you don't understand the latter, you will overdetermine the significance of the former. What we can't do is presume that the map or the archive is an objective record of anything. They are always ideological arguments – but they contain multiple ideological arguments, they're never singular. We have to understand them as multi-dimensional texts where Indigenous and Black and Afro-Indigenous and otherwise marginalised people are demonstrating a kind of presence; an assertion of a presence, even in its vexedness. Allotment maps were also an attempt to individualise and fix collective tribal being, so by understanding them as multi-dimensional, mapping change across time, we can also see a collective resistance to the individualisation of allotment.

The allotment maps aren't just geographic maps: they're kinship maps, they're relational maps. They have people's names on them, and kin tried to get their allotments near one another, so then you start to understand relationships. We can read a lot of things through these maps, but you also have to have a lot of context and some understanding of kinship relations to understand that they're never just static documents. They weren't composed at one time: they are rolling documents historicising kinship relations, but also kinship fragmentations.

I call them cartographic kinscapes. The kin part is really important, but it's not self-evident. There are all kinds of ways that these maps become stories, or potential stories, or erase particular kinds of stories. If you don't have context, you can create a very limited narrative around the maps that simplifies Cherokee survivors, that flattens out the complexity of our nationhood. And there's a lot of complexity in those maps: some of them identify Cherokee Freedmen, they identify newborns, there are some cemeteries on those maps. When we look at a lot of those allotment lands now, we see most of them are out of Cherokee hands; we can actually see the material and relational losses. That's a lot of people who are trying to figure out where their great-grandparents lived and where their family was from. These maps help us ground those relations and show the network of relations that we've been severed from.

So mapping has helped me be more attentive to kinship, but because kinship is not linear, it's four-dimensional, you also have to start thinking of the maps differently. I may have been a bit more literal with the maps before I started more focused kinship research and conversations. Now I see the maps as having dimensionality to them, or at least anticipating dimensions and being used to articulate dimensionality.

SM: That sense of temporality – of maps having the dimensionality of space*time* – seems crucial. Le Guin's maps for her early novel *Planet of Exile* were of seasonal shifts, not just static geography. And the relation between the map of the Melded World and, over the page, the inset map of the Everland in *The Kynship Chronicles* is also a notation of temporality and temporal change, of the encroachment of colonisation.

DHJ: When I was working on the trilogy, I was doing a lot of reading on pre-colonial Cherokee territories, and what the environment looked like: how built up it was, how inhabited it was. We were not in an Eden, we were in a living land! How alien that was, and how hard it was to imagine, even for somebody who was a lifelong fantasy reader and whose motto is 'Imagine otherwise'! I was really challenged to think: why am I having a hard time seeing this in my imagination? Part of the point of the trilogy was to challenge myself to imagine a world where we existed in our own sovereign realities, in all the conflicts and complications of that, before we were so violently defined by and through the settler imaginary. And that was a really humbling exercise.

During the revisions, *1491* by Charles C Mann came out and, although it's a great book, what was sad was that it was such a revelation. The fascination that thoughtful readers had with it was great, but there was also such a deep reactionary response of settler anxiety with the idea that there was something really meaningful and sophisticated and complicated here that was intentionally and systematically destroyed. Colonial societies work with the assumption that they impose the only true meaning, so the idea that genuine and even more wondrous meaning pre-existed them is an existential threat to settler superiority.

Every colonial society seeks to destroy the meaning that precedes its violent arrival. Then any attempts to recover and uncover that that previous meaning, or ongoing meaning, have to be violently responded to. We're seeing that in the United States, in the resurgence of the banning of books and the destruction of archives. That's a pathological fear response. It's strategic as well, but it's deeply rooted. The point of *The Kynship Chronicles* was to interrogate that mindset, not so much focusing on colonisers, but on Indigenous subjects. With the Everland map, I wanted readers to have an intimacy with that area, so that when the expulsion of the Darkening Road happened, they felt it.

Even for folks who are very invested in anticolonial action, it's sometimes very hard to imagine who we were before. That was part of the exercise for me, and it was more challenging than I realised. The Everland is this glorious, gorgeous place, but even then it's a place that's been changed. We learn by the end that the *whole world* was ours. The People were the entirety of the map, not just a fragment. It belonged to the various Folk, but their imaginations had shrunk as peril encroached. At the end they realise: it's not that this little bit is ours. We've been gaslit into believing that is all that remains, but everything was ours.

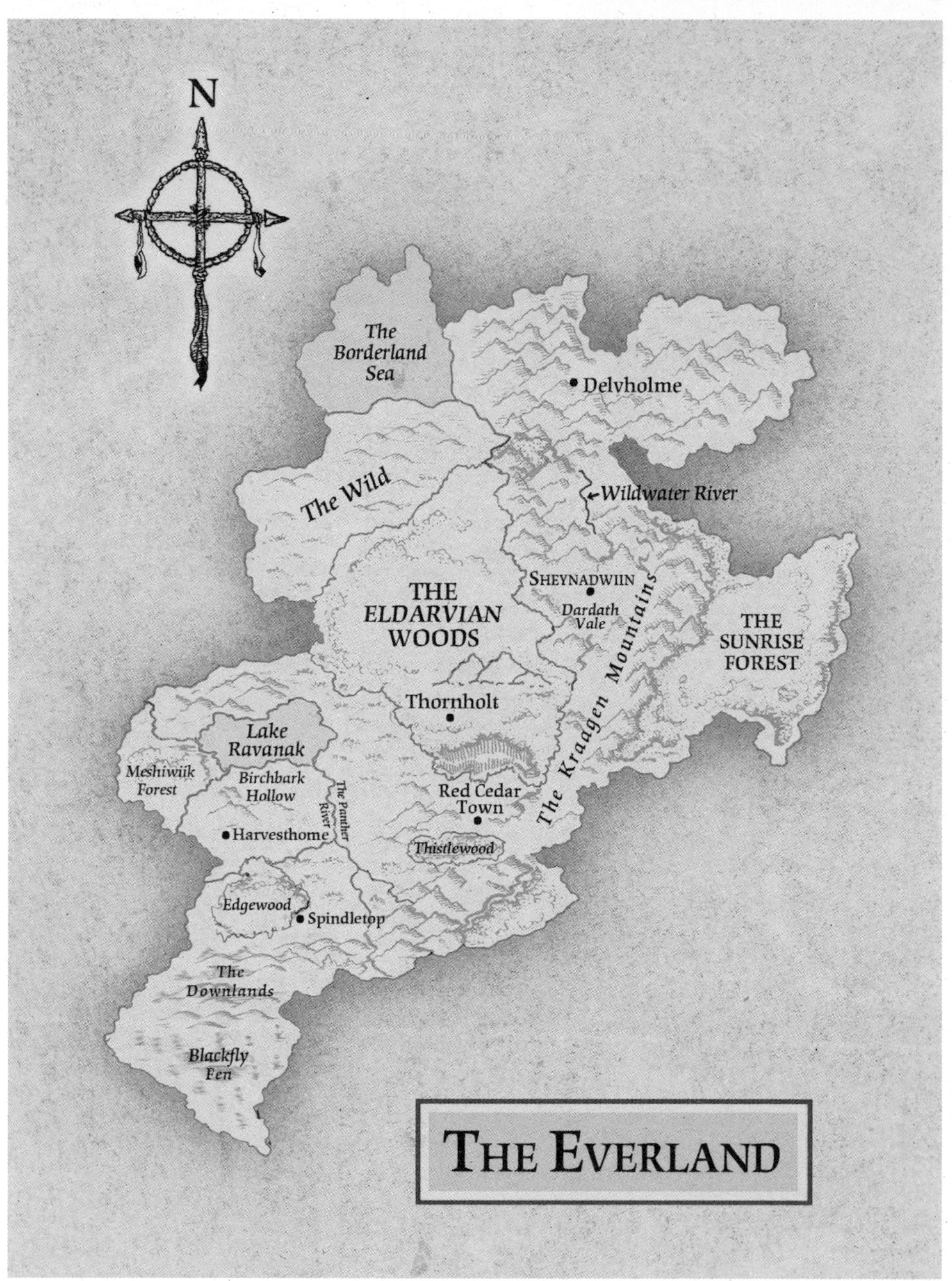

The Everland, published in *The Way of Thorn and Thunder: The Kynship Chronicles* by Daniel Heath Justice (2011)

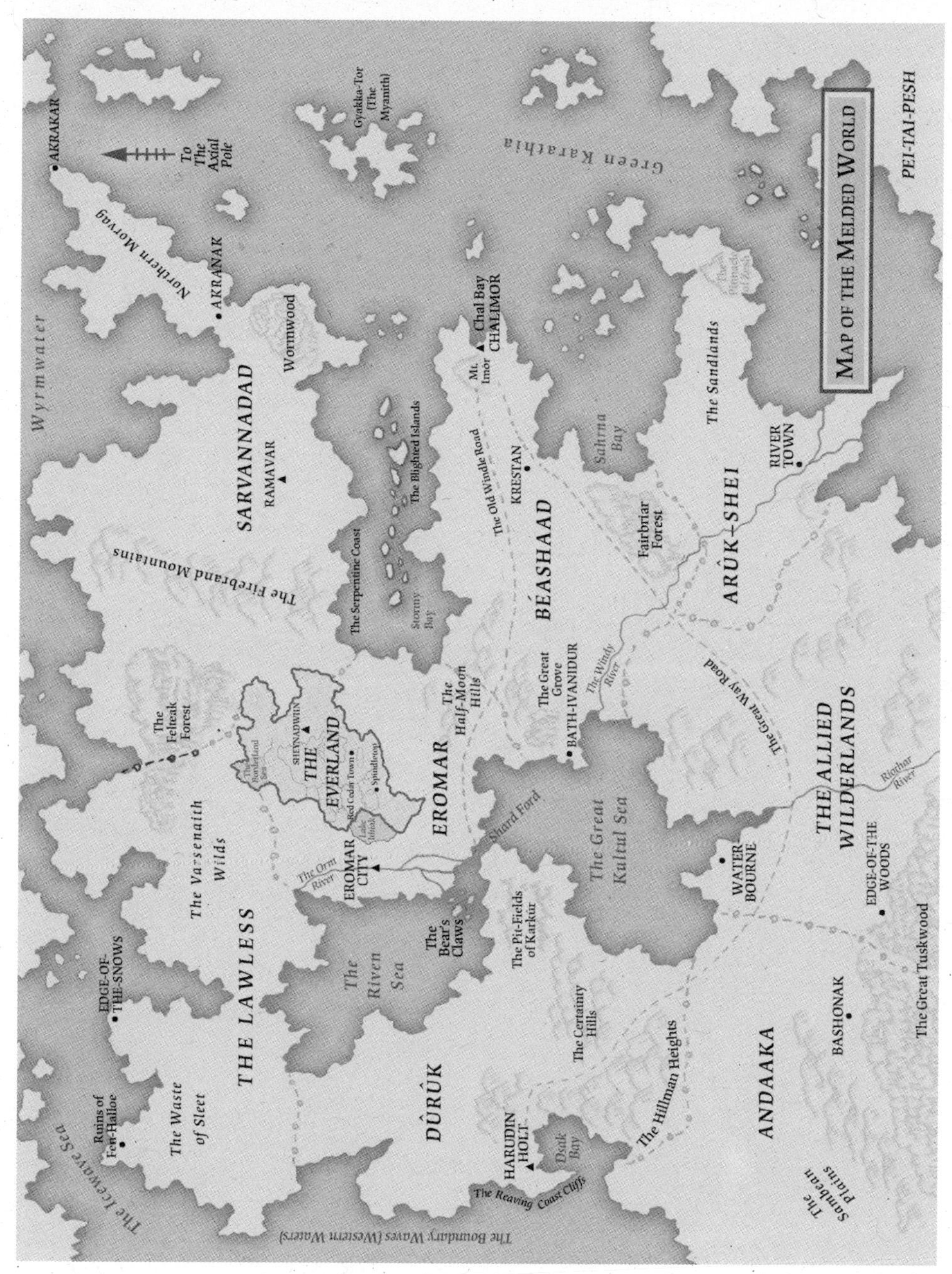

Map of the Melded World, published in *The Way of Thorn and Thunder: The Kynship Chronicles* by Daniel Heath Justice (2011)

60

They sat on the floor. Very gently, Rolly picked up the alien's limp hand, letting it lie on her own, which looked white, + fragile against the broad, bony, well-muscled Dinconid hand with its covering of brown fur as fine + close as a silken glove.

The world is a satellite of a 2-lqs dead planet, whose phases (full-full) take 360 24-hour days. These are the time-divisions corresp to earth-year; 60 of them to a Year. Plane of the ecliptic scarcely tilted.

Each season 15 yrs

Tides & earthquakes wd be pretty terrific

fall
summer
fast
slow
winter
spring
Midsummer
summer
15
30
fall
winter
45
spring
New Year
midwinter

Diagram of seasons on Werel, unpublished, for *Planet of Exile* (1966).

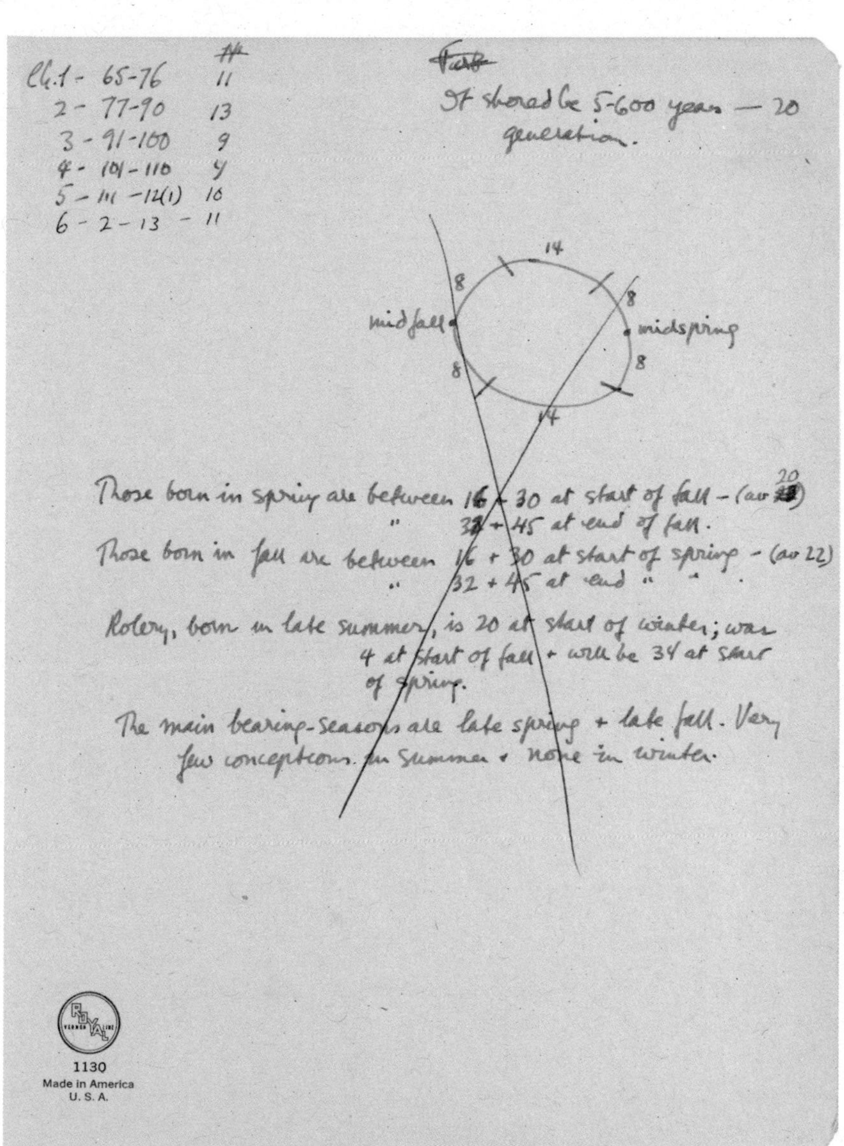

		#
Ch. 1 -	65-76	11
2 -	77-90	13
3 -	91-100	9
4 -	101-110	4
5 -	111 - 12(1)	10
6 -	2 - 13 -	11

It should be 5-600 years — 20 generation.

Those born in spring are between 16 + 30 at start of fall - (av 20)
" 32 + 45 at end of fall.
Those born in fall are between 16 + 30 at start of spring - (av 22)
" 32 + 45 at end " " .

Rolery, born in late summer, is 20 at start of winter; was 4 at start of fall + will be 34 at start of spring.

The main bearing-seasons are late spring + late fall. Very few conceptions in summer + none in winter.

Diagram of seasons on Werel, unpublished, for *Planet of Exile* (1966).

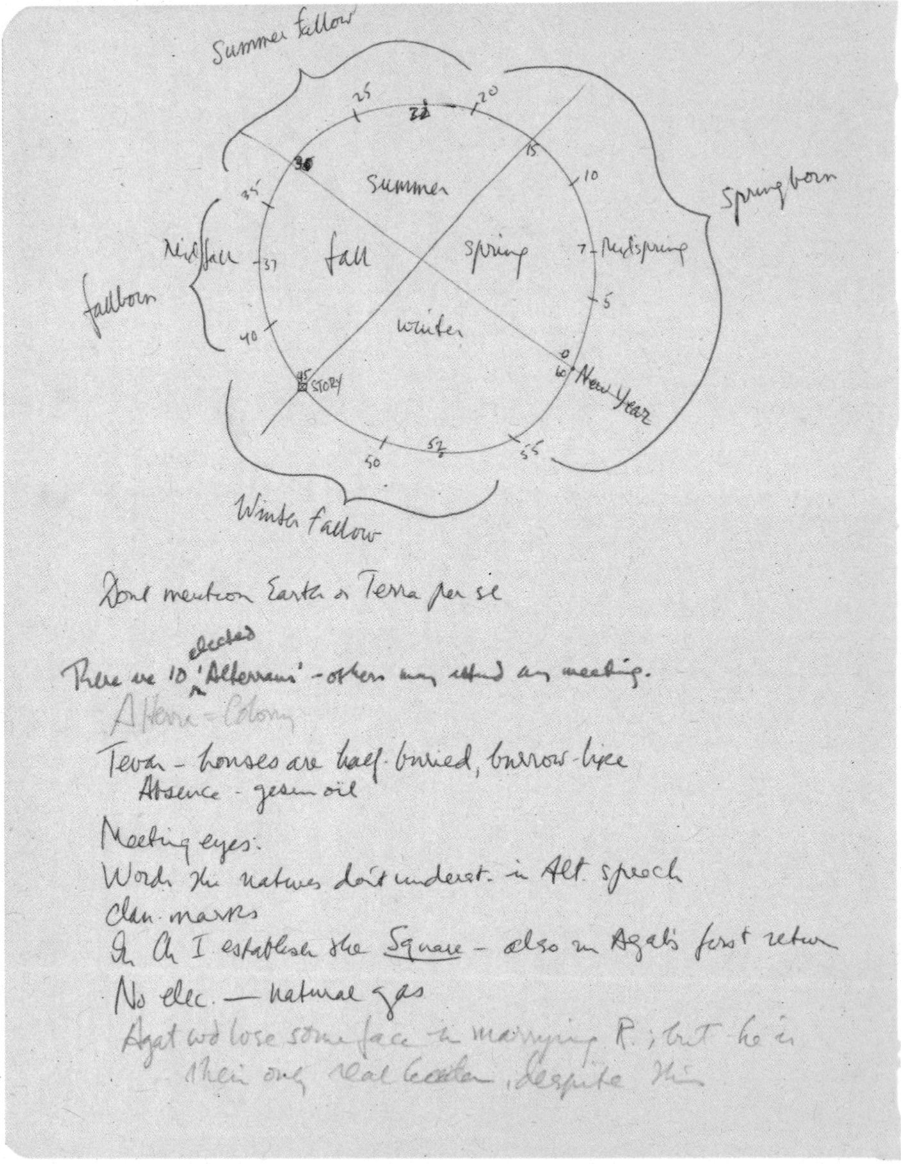

Summer fallow

25 22 20

15

30 Summer 10

35 Springborn

Midfall 37 fall spring 7 Midspring

fallborn 5

40 winter

0

60 New Year

45 STORY

50 52 55

Winter fallow

Don't mention Earth or Terra per se

There are 10 elected 'Alterrans' - others may attend any meeting.

Alterra = Colony

Tevar - houses are half-buried, burrow-like

Absence - gesm oil

Meeting eyes:

Words the natives don't underst. in Alt. speech

Clan-marks

In Ch I establish the Square - also in Agat's first return

No elec. — natural gas

Agat wd lose some face in marrying R.; but he is their only real leader, despite this

Diagram of seasons on Werel, unpublished,
for *Planet of Exile* (1966).

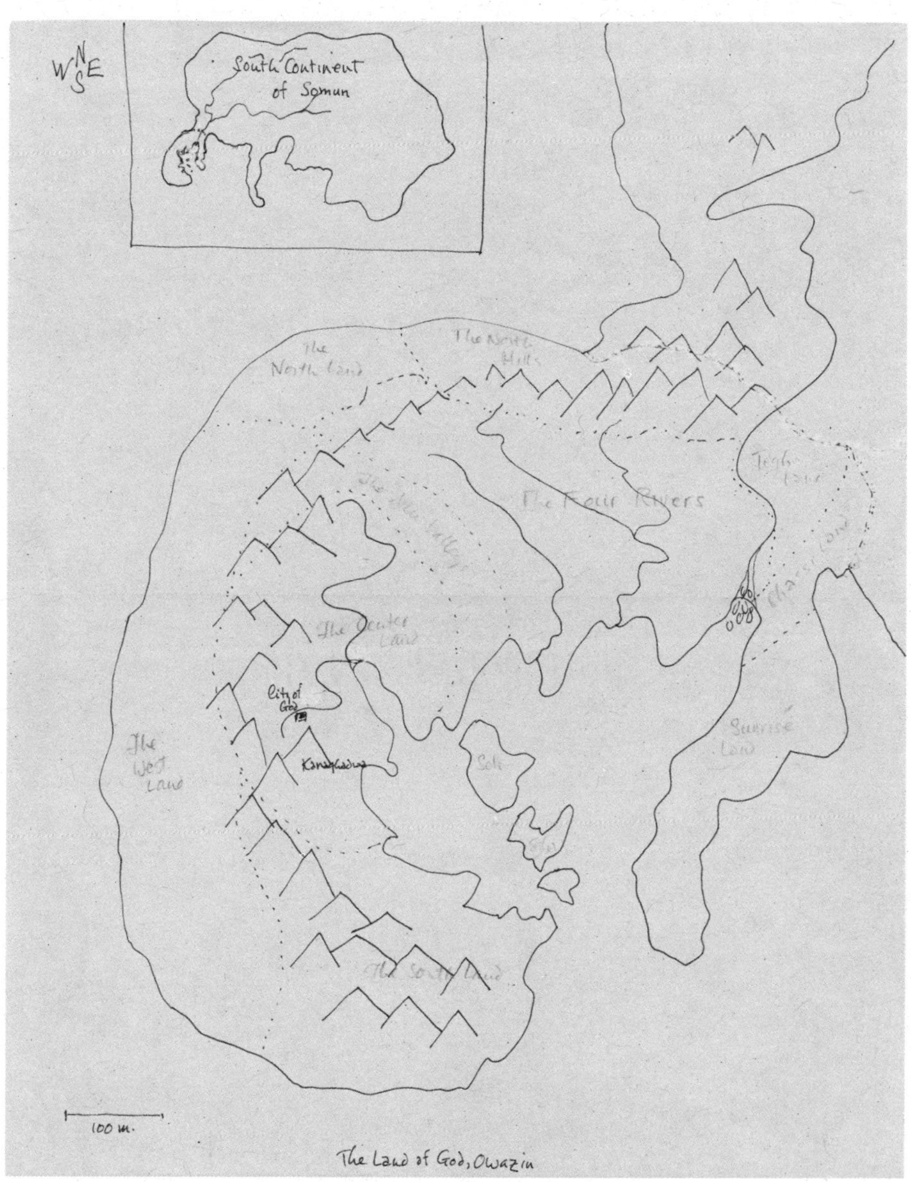

The Land of God, Owazin, unpublished,
for *The Birthday of the World* (2002).

2

A cold planet, almost seasonless; a great red-brown moon. Habitable only to 40° N + S of equator. Electric power est. in the most advanced countries, Karhide and Orgoreyn: a long slow industrial age, now 1500 years old — things are very established + durable.

Geog:

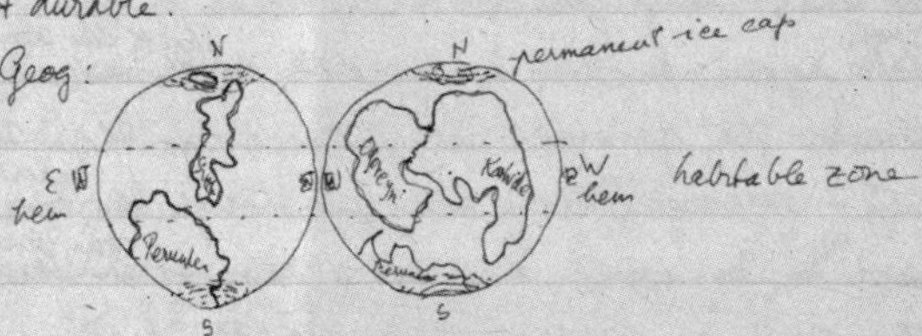

Terrain: Mountainous in Karhide, cut w river-valleys, leading to considerable local autonomy; the W. of the country is flatter, running to the rich plains of Orgoreyn; the Kingship arose from a dynasty that first drove out the Orgota, + h maintained the boundaries ever since. Power, coal, lumber fr. the W. mts., but food (mainly grains + fruit + root-veg.) fr that disputed ~~western~~ plain.

Grains were imported by the Hainish Settlers along w men; there are no large graminivores; no lg carnivores; no mammals, only semi-placentals + various egg-protecting devices. No birds; cold-blooded forms are v. primitive; 'fish' are warm-blooded. Fish + fish-eggs are much eaten but meat of land animals is only wild game + small.

The first map of Gethen, unpublished, for 'Winter's King', *Orbit* (September 1969).

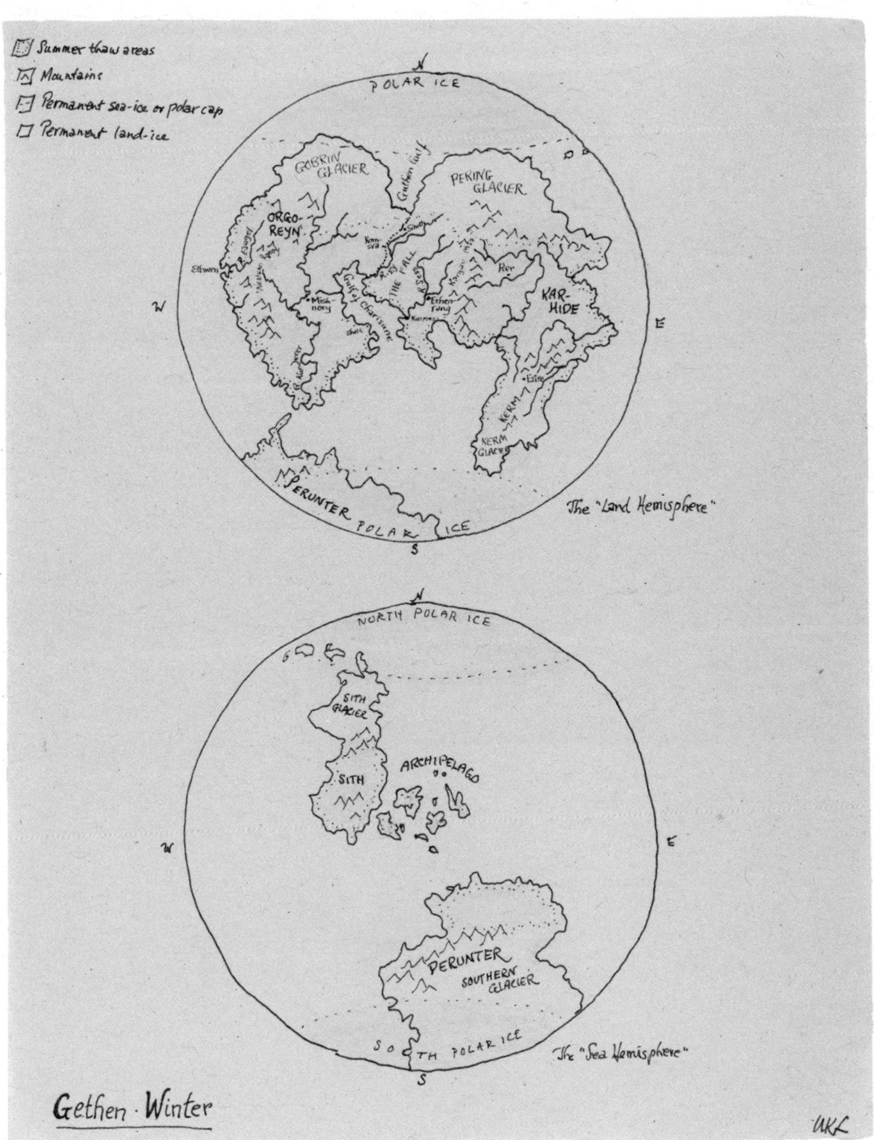

Hemispheres of Gethen, unpublished,
for *The Left Hand of Darkness* (1969).

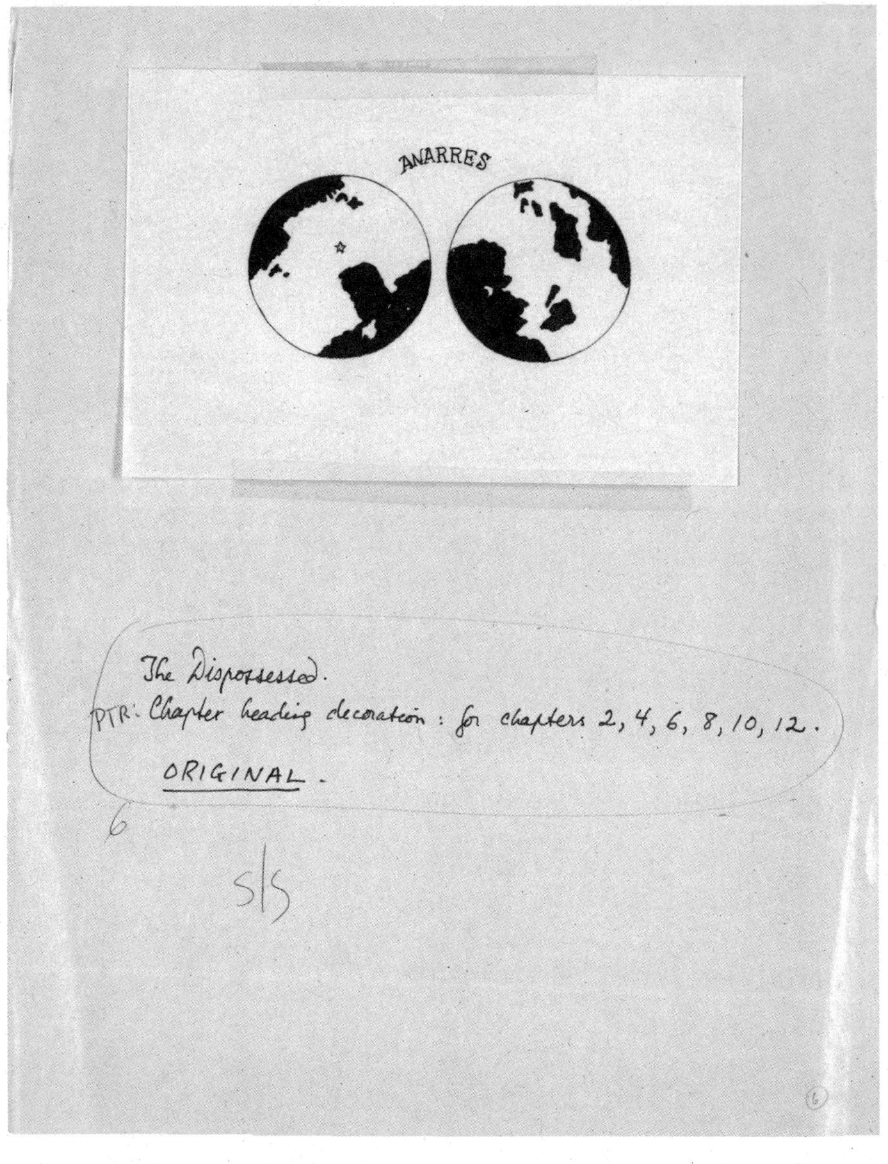

Anarres chapter head, published in *The Dispossessed* (1974).

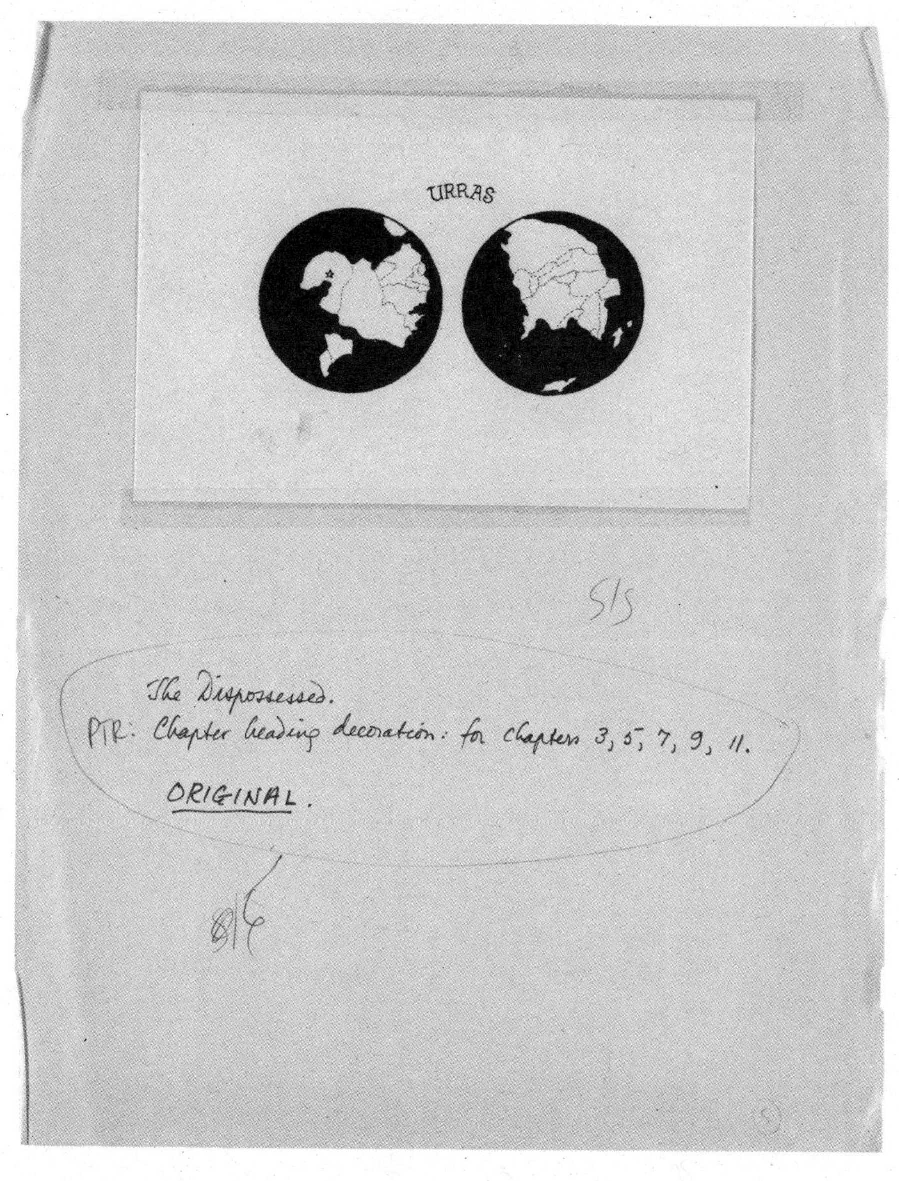

Urras chapter head, published in *The Dispossessed* (1974).

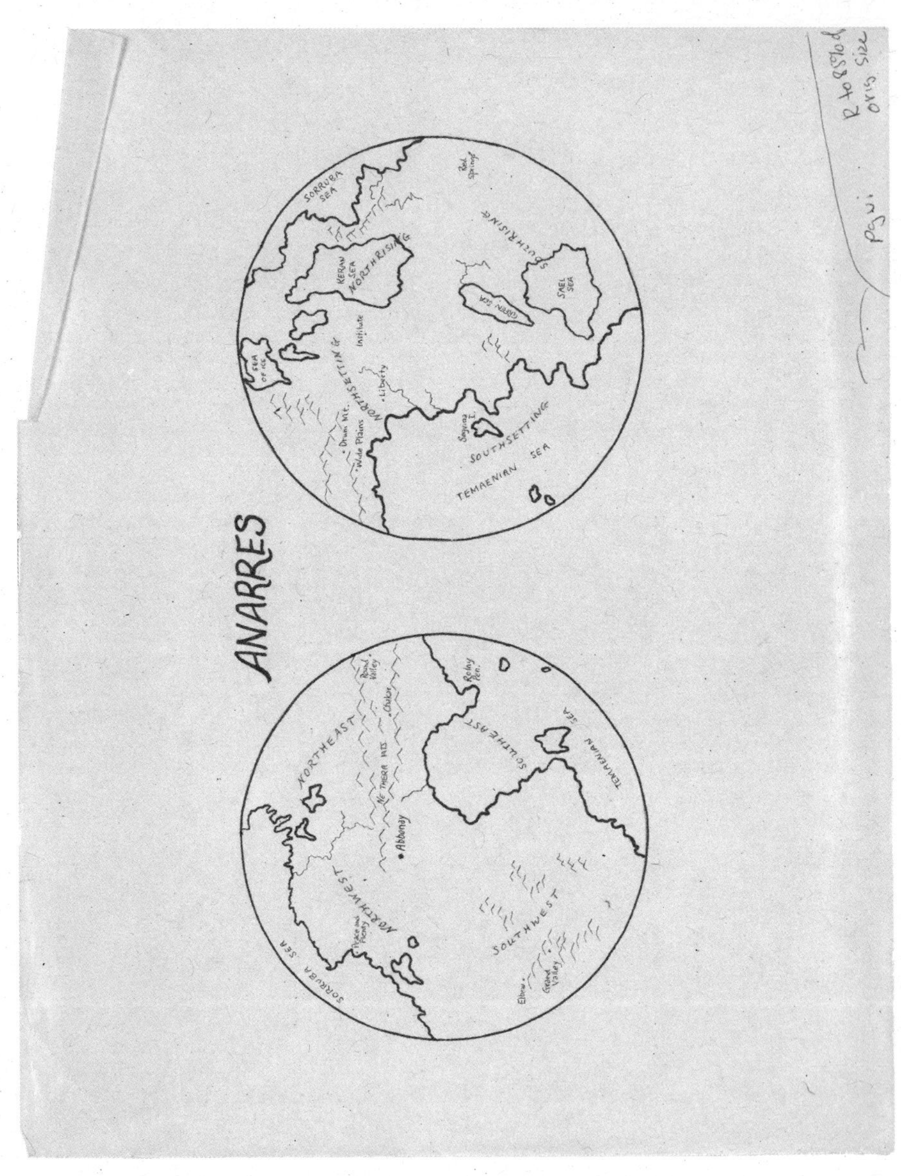

Hemispheres of Anarres, published in *The Dispossessed* (1974).

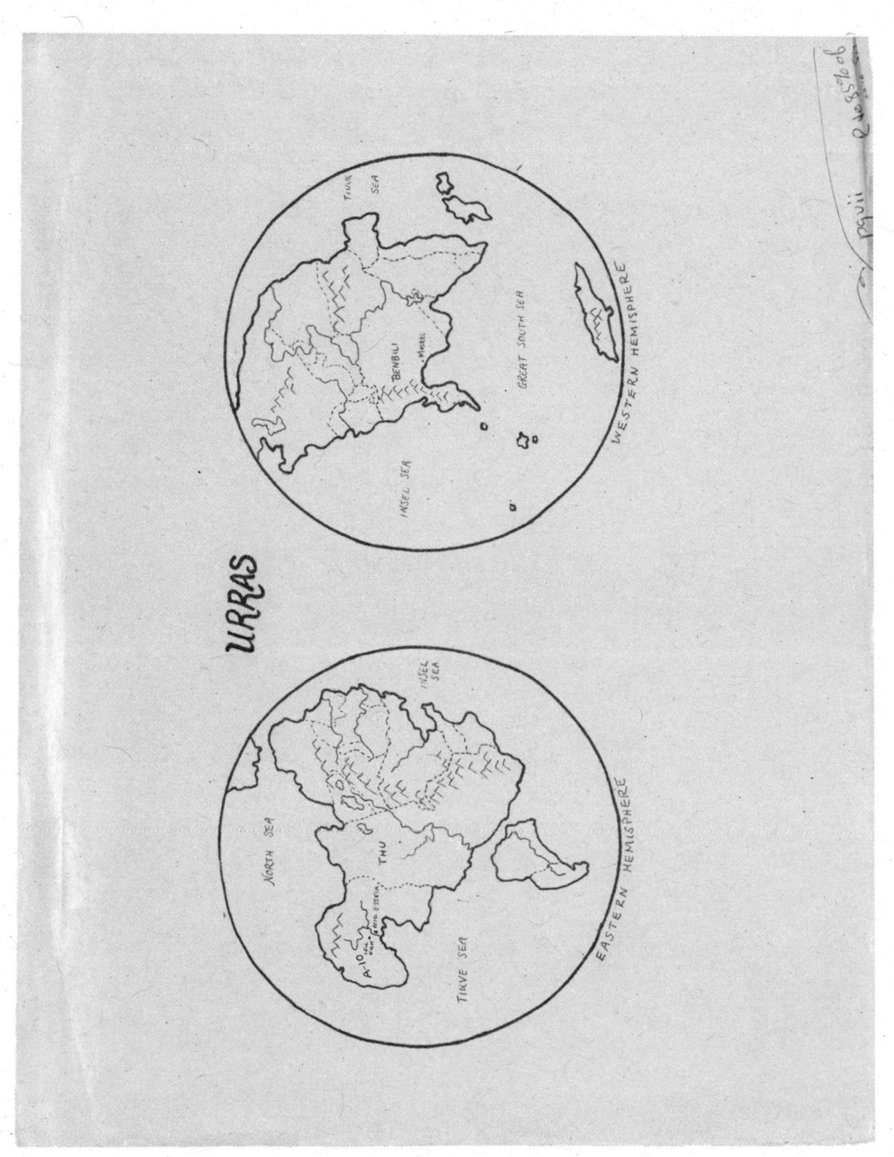

Hemispheres of Urras, published in *The Dispossessed* (1974).

Una McCormack

The Dark Passages of the Mind

Seen from above, the map of the labyrinth at Chartres Cathedral resembles the folds and curls of the human brain. Measured and regular, this is an orderly mind; surely any pilgrimage through these passages would be purposeful and meditative, bringing clarity of thought. (Indeed, maze-walking has been picked up by practitioners of mindfulness as yet another means of mitigating against the complexities of contemporary life.)

On the London Underground, that frenetic subterranean web of complex interconnections, a multi-part work by Mark Wallinger has seen the installation of 270 individual labyrinth artworks – one at each Tube station. They're intended as an invitation to travellers to stop and trace their way through the maze, removing themselves from the hustle of the Tube. They offer a moment of quiet and order as the trains and the crowds press past; an exercise of control over oneself and one's environment.

Next to these, the Labyrinth of the Tombs of Atuan appears to be a place of chaos and confusion. The passages do not arrange themselves into a pleasing overall design. They turn cunningly and you must find your way through in darkness. There are pits and traps and shallow graves. *The Tombs of Atuan*, second in the young adult fantasy Earthsea series, concerns the coming-to-maturity of Tenar, taken as a young girl to become the high priestess of the 'Nameless Ones' at a temple complex located in a remote desert region of the island of Atuan. Beneath the complex lies the Labyrinth; part of Tenar's religious training consists of learning her way through its unlit winding corridors.

The two maps that Le Guin drew for the novel (p 28–9) do not line up, and it took me longer to realise this than does me credit; they're upside-down in relation to each other, so that as you try to lay one on top of the other, as you attempt to connect the overground to down-below, you have to perform a secondary mental transformation. This, surely, is a mind in disarray. But the labyrinth of Atuan has a purpose, and it is the opposite of those real-world examples which aim to bring order and mental clarity:

> It was wonderful, laid out in the solid rock underground like the streets of a great city; but it had been made to weary and confuse the mortal walking in it, and even its priestess must feel it to be nothing, in the end, but a great trap.[1]

In *The Tombs of Atuan*, Tenar's own experience of learning the labyrinth is double-edged: it gives her a sense of mastery and of independence (particularly from her rival, the cruel priestess Kossil):

> She did not go far into [the Labyrinth] that first time, but far enough that the strange, bitter, yet pleasurable certainty of her utter solitude and independence there grew strong in her, and led her back, and back again, and each time farther.[2]

But the secrets she learns are in service to malignant others. This is freedom constrained. You may only walk on the designated pathways.

Yet that 'solitude and independence' are precisely what open up the space for something new, something different. A critical conversation with her friend Penthe – while eating apples, no less – reveals to Tenar the possibility of non-belief, of 'unfaith'. The priestess Thar, the closest Tenar has to a mother figure, teaches her how religion and politics are knotted together, how ritual is tangled up in hierarchy, in power plays and social control. Into this growing gap, Ged's magelight shines, presenting Tenar with a vision of another world; another way of being in the world; another route out:

> To have seen the Undertomb confused her; she was bewildered ... She had seen it, and the mystery had given place, not to horror, but to beauty, a mystery deeper even than that of the dark.[3]

When I first read *The Tombs of Atuan*, sometime in the early 1980s, I was on the threshold of adolescence, a precipice that is daunting enough without living in a

Catholic household far closer in spirit to the 1950s than the 1980s. If school was *Just Seventeen* and Judy Blume, home meant weekly Mass and family rosaries; May processions and Stations of the Cross; giving-up-for-Lent and Lourdes holy water. The long haul of Holy Week and the Good Friday service, with its rituals and incense and bleak chants. (No dances in the dark of night, sadly. No juggling with knives.) These ancient and (in many ways) comforting rituals were radicalised by my Irish family's sense of rebellion against external rule, but were still, for me, increasingly imbued with an overwhelming sense of suffocation; the sense that something was being buried alive.

Into this rather narrow pre-adolescence, *The Tombs of Atuan* landed like a depth charge. It was a Puffin edition, with a whitewashed Ged on the cover, not Tenar – a double decentring. 'Intersectional' wasn't in my lexicon back then; I don't think I even noticed. I read and reread the book many times during my teens. It's obvious what the attraction must have been for a thoughtful adolescent girl receiving mixed messages about obedience to rule and the romance of revolution. The presence of a female protagonist alone was enough to make the book worthy of my repeated attention. Yet its impact was apparently negligible. I remained a practising Catholic for much longer than one might imagine. I did leave, in the end – a major earthquake felt only by me, followed by a thoroughly deep depression, from which, in time, I did emerge:

> Her despair grew so great that it burst her breast open and like a bird of fire shattered the stone and broke out into the light of day – the light of day, faint in her windowless room.[4]

Feminist science fiction, graduate study, making friends and connections who opened up my mind to whole new worlds and words (intersectionality, not least); half a lifetime of reading and reflecting and responding has followed. But *The Tombs of Atuan* worked an early and deep spell on me, one that I did not recognise at the time. In retrospect, I see that it offered me a map to psychological terrain that I didn't even know I was inhabiting, laying out routes to new territory and reworking pathways in my brain. It offered me the taste of sweet apples from the tree of knowledge; it handed me a ball of tangled thread and said, 'Where, do you think, might this take you? What might you make of it?'

> 'You are free, Tenar,' [said Ged]. 'You were taught to be a slave, but you have broken free.'[5]

1 Le Guin, *The Tombs of Atuan* (Puffin Books, 1974), p 62.
2 Ibid, p 52.
3 Ibid, p 67.
4 Ibid, p 103–4.
5 Ibid, p 114.

Marilyn Strathern

World Maps : Word Maps

If maps of islands first spring to mind from Ursula K Le Guin's sketches, perhaps it is because the sea is such a potent connector. It was by sea that I first travelled to the world's second largest island, the landmass of New Guinea (east and west). Upon hearing of my trip, the artist Evelyn Simpson – a family friend – depicted New Guinea in oils, the whole no more than the size of my hand. Set in choppy waters, the island rises to a volcanic peak that emerges out of dense green and brightly flowering foliage, a bird of paradise visible in the lower reaches, a hut approached by a high path, the shore surrounding all with coconut palms and broad sands. The painting is not so much what she imagined New Guinea might be like, rather a miniaturisation of certain elemental-mythical details. There's not a person in sight, only ominous driftwood in the foreground.

How is an island to be peopled? For this is the task of the social anthropologist. Every place is an island in this sense. I look at the lands of Earthsea; regions are named, archipelagoes are named, every land of any size is named. People, too, are there in the words for these places, and even a cursory glance reveals different linguistic formations. There would be no concept of travelling if one couldn't ask: where am I now?

Beginning with words

The peopling of an island begins with words: with questions from those travellers who make landfall. New arrivals, archetypal outsiders, would assume that inhabited places are named. They might not be able to make head or tail of what they are told, or might make heads from tails as in the designations that enshrine ancient misunderstandings. '[You should go] over there!' Is it too much to presume that travellers' preoccupation with sea charts, or the potential maps already forming in their head, could lead them to imagine that the first things people say are where they are, or what they are called? Perhaps, but at the same time, the etiquette of naming is also part of travellers' tales, and no one should be surprised by those that remain hidden or unspoken, or by grasping – as the Wizard of Earthsea quickly did – that utterance is also power. The last thing people might say are their own names.

Questions and answers are in themselves the trickiest of interlocutions, as Genly Ai finds during his time on Gethen (*The Left Hand of Darkness*, 1969), in trying to understand his companion Estraven. What is said in deference or irony, or what is even utterable or unutterable, are matters not only of language learning but of expectation and convention. In some areas of New Guinea, it was once an expression of empathy to ask what was making a person so angry that they had fallen sick. Where people loved to compute things, as was true of much of Indigenous New Guinea, an outsider could formulate questions about quantity, crucial for reckoning up debts and credits or who could be counted on for support. By the same token, charting the ever-changing constellations of local groups depended on who was included or excluded, and – as when two parents could differ in the 'number' of children they said they had – outside interrogators might reach the limits of their own numerical logic. Here the certainty of government census takers was a marvel to behold, especially in the eyes of those New Guineans whose collectivities included the dead among the living.

Like the line between light and dark, or left and right hand, that relationship between living and dead could shimmer between being almost absolute and almost non-existent. Each elicited the presence of the other, as anger (ideally) elicited empathy. Time and again Le Guin comes back to duality. Indeed, her novels and short stories touch on numerous different ways of thinking and naming in pairs and opposites. This is where her own maps and their directions come in.

To Le Guin's explicit reference to yin and yang in *The Left Hand of Darkness*, one is tempted to add the duality of any encounter between persons. Whether between a person's states of being or among interlocutors or from one inhabited world to another, distance emerges as a basic trope of travelling. Thus created, this distance requires mapping: a means of connection-direction. Mapping requires observation, which makes the worlds of observer and observed appear at once strange and yet familiar to each other. Is that also true of writing and being written about? Or of the third party-relationship between author or subject and reader, whose mutual medium (the sea in which they swim) is largely the word?

Wordless interlocutors

Much has happened since Le Guin embarked on her voyages. In exploring the limits set by specific existential conditions, she deliberately remained within Earth's orbit: however altered in this or that respect, she invariably found some counterpart to people, human or hominid. Of course, given the reach of her curiosity, any generalisation is hazardous, and she did visit a world of no people, in 'Vaster than Empires and More Slow' (1971).[1] Within Earth's orbit, like Le Guin, anthropologists have for some time been exploring inter-species and other 'other-than-human' lives.

This has meant abandoning words as a medium of encounter, although not of course in the third party relationship with readers. Ray Nayler's *The Mountain in the Sea* (2022) draws from an anthropological account of how forests think,[2] and deals with investigators' symbolic, though wordless, communications with an Earth 'alien', the octopus. Many other elements of encounter are there, including the ultimate realisation that the observed was also an observer. However, the novel engages in an elaborate verbal address to the reader. While set in a not so distant dystopian future that makes for a plausible plot, each chapter is prefaced by explanatory abstracts (distilled from the author's extensive reading into communication and consciousness): they appear as brief excerpts from two quasi-scientific accounts written by the main protagonist and the obsessed researcher who co-opts her into an experiment.

These fragments within the text give verisimilitude to the way in which knowledge unfolds for the reader.

Le Guin has used similar devices – field notes, diaries, reports – whether to inform a portion of narrative or to sharpen an alternative perspective, thereby condensing information too awkward to emerge in passing. But for the most part her narratives themselves carry forward any investigative or exploratory enlargements of the reader's comprehension. The directions are given by what we could call her word-maps.

Word-maps

The diverse journeys on which Le Guin takes the reader are frequently cued by certain phrasings or word plays. These map out a problematic by pointing to a something still in the distance of any grasp on things or by landing the reader in an unexpected place. Above all, her word-maps provide another perspective on where a reader thought they were.

Thus, the most overt pun – as in the short stories under *Changing Planes* (2002) – can work as a charm to suspend familiar connections and allow other connections to emerge (incidentally, these include a story about people whose language, in appearing not to name anything, defies all translation). It makes one wonder how often Le Guin suspends stereotypes in the same way, whether or not she is drawing attention to them. It is almost as though the planet (the 'island') of Athshe (*The World for World is Forest*, 1972) was deliberately peopled by 'little green men'.[3] The reader first encounters them through the dismissiveness of a colonial character who, for all his contemporary political resonance, is also stereotypical. Then there is the internal strategy of dropping into the beginning of a tale a concept that is initially unexplained, but becomes a reference point to which there is constant return. The *kemmer* experienced by Gethenians in *The Left Hand of Darkness* must be the most famous example, upending conventional patterns of sexual reproduction and gender roles.

However, through the layering of her plots, Le Guin's words also divert the reader, revealing and disguising other directions, so that what is mapped out is not quite what it seems.

So, that world of no people. In 'Vaster than Empires and More Slow', the bickering and antagonisms of the travellers to World 4470 seem to hold the plot. In their claustrophobic spaceship, this is especially true of the hatred generated by an excessively sensitive crew member, the closest to an alien, an outcast. The world they have come to survey is a stark contrast to their own. Yet, it is only at the end of the story that the reader realises this world does not lack conscious beings: it lacks the dualisms that *human* consciousness produces. The planet itself is a single sentient being, with no experience of aliens, just a sense of itself without a sense of an other. In other words, the dualisms that seemed over-determining in Gethen are elsewhere variables encountered in their absence. Or take the few pages of 'The Nna Mmoy Language' (2002) that give us the language of no names.[4] The reader is lulled into a description of this dull, safe place where everything is useful and only the language is impossible to comprehend. People write texts, listen raptly to one another, apparently recite poetry, but visitors cannot talk with them. It seems like just another variation on what we know. The twist at the end comes from something Le Guin has explored before: that all of this (variation) is the outcome of (human) experimentation. In this place, it was decided to eliminate anything that does not have a rational use. But be careful what you wish for: the residents' resistance lay in an endlessly complicated and infinitely rich language that defied mapping onto other people's tongues.

Maps inside out

However they travel to their islands of study, anthropologists arrive with maps already in their heads. The numerous named, described and analysed locations that their colleagues have studied are often miniaturised into what they all call theories, which can be carried in hand baggage as toolkits and concepts. These include the concept that the concepts they come with may well be overturned in some way. In truth, early voyagers often brought nomenclatures with them – their maps recorded the lands they expected to find, or the names of monarchs or explorers. An anthropologist's language comes at once as a medium of communication and a great encumbrance to it. If you have recorded an encounter where one person asks another, 'Are you dead or alive?', you know there is more going on than the words you hear.

It would be a fallacy of course to equate islands with inevitable isolation. New Guinea is a place of many places, within and beyond it, whether in relation to one another or to the rest of the world. The island is connected through flows of all kinds, material and immaterial, and not least through the sea of words on which people forever set sail. Anthropologists have endlessly unpicked the metaphor of travelling, in order to prick the myth of new arrival, with all the temporal and spatial alienation that implies. That said, in a particularly potent way, Le Guin's enchanting drawings still talk back to anthropology.

Perhaps there is a sense in which anthropologists have to externalise the word-maps in their heads. To be open and responsive to shifting situations, it may help to perceive one's theories and concepts – embodied in the words that carry them – as to some extent on the outside, like an external cloak or carapace. Even if escape is not completely possible, one can at least peer out from underneath the veil. In plotting the universe of regions and locations that were to unfold in her narratives, Le Guin externalised her world map. It was necessary to lay out the coordinates of where in the world, or in which world, this or that story was located. For in the guise of characters able to move from one place to another, what Le Guin seemingly wanted to shift were the visions of those conditions of existence that elicited certain responses and compelled certain actions. If your world only yields up the useful, what resources are left to play with?

Acknowledgements
Thanks to both James Leach and Alan Strathern for enlarging my reading.

1 Le Guin, 'Vaster Than Empires and More Slow', first published in *New Dimensions 1*, edited by Robert Silverberg (Doubleday, 1971), republished in *The Wind's Twelve Quarters* (Harper & Row, 1975) and *The Compass Rose* (Gollancz, 2015), pp 167–201.

2 Eduardo Kohn, *How Forests Think: Toward an Anthropology Beyond the Human* (University of California Press, 2013).

3 'I wrote *The Little Green Men* (its first editor, Harlan Ellison, retitled it, with my rather morose permission) in the winter of 1968', Le Guin, 'Introduction to *The Word for World is Forest* (1977)', *The Language of the Night: Essays on Fantasy and Science Fiction*, edited by Susan Wood and revised by Le Guin, (The Women's Press, 1989), p 127.

4 Le Guin, 'The Nna Mmoy Language', in *Changing Planes* (Gollancz, 2004), pp 144–56.

Canisia Lubrin

-.-. .... . -.-. -.- .--. --- .. -. - / ....- .---- / -.--. .---- -.... - .... / -.-. .-.-.- -.--.-

ATTN: CHECKPOINT 41 (~~16th C~~)

Again, the evening child is shadow-hearted and somehow
Nobody blooms a gutted grace partial to her February.
To penknives, skins, the foundry is someone's surprising life.
Please excuse my parole. I desire to be again defenceless

Before Orcas fourteen days adrift. Calf per bewailed calf. The future
A figure of speech and two lifetimes of extinctions, all paper-wise
Seal my mouth. The Lede, for once, admits the coming storm. Feeds
What pinhole mouths will log. The bric-a-brac astrologers giving
No creed enough for the harbour. For the door to this electric world.

Of barcode plagues. Hungry sight. Empty myself. As the voicebox rears
An anticlimax I must disappoint with glances. Cotton blouses flown
Over mass graves. Let's buy us passage then, with a newly traded life.
Before others: a crowd-sourced end, a city stripped of its bright petals.
When the cemetery with the CA$H-4-GOLD billboard is the tyrant's.
Who outbids us what life, these vaster shoulders uphill, 1 part-per-billion.

And now we are lizard-tongued, unmasked as you. *Mélangé sa mélangé.*

What is invisible tonight is overhearing. Gramsci in 'the time
Of monsters'. And to be pleased with apologies. Harmless tools.
With a shovel for this vision of the world. Its wrecked airs tested in
Saltwater. Formaldehydes for what I've said. What I won't come to.

Everywhere. This naked rift between my phrases dissolves, stunned
By sudden worry. Yet art is the seaward stone. Cast left. At lamps.
Right at animals. White as the clock. Clock of rules. Linkups icy here
In the telescope's selfing. I am no bidder, caretaker, warner of Gold
Coasts, paved for begging magnates, saddled in our small deaths.

Only now could a glad of arbannes be new as fines. That immolation
Should've been a poem. 'god sent me, give me all...' We do not kill
To resolve our differences – 'dread, this is a stick-up'. Everywhere.
Another life eases the ruins. Who is killed minus knife. Minus deeds.
What new distance between tired histories. And times of rout am I.
Alone with the healer, bossman. I fly from this end in electronic mail.

Searching everywhere you walk. You're invited out. Of this last frame.

Alright. Let us meet in the convoy, hunger-void and fine.
With new names for needs. Anything we'll eat in the daylight.
Anything blue and scorching. Set here before all error or escape.
Bright ribbons for the war-torn broods. Our shaggy bait for bonfire.

For the crossness of original survivors to I, who can fix to. You.
All (un)fleshed. Sculptures. Vacancies. The breaking newsfeed.
A trilling Golden Horde inside a louvre. A Wall-Street-Black-Death.
New (w)age for the girl's symbol of a god's hatching toward god-
shaped.
Who comes cleanly to this bright brigade. This opalescent shade.

Note the shape of love in her border tent, disappearing the legal code.
East to north, 1804, 2023. Search us this upright. Ash in a stiff wind.
Spores in my misshapen ear. They've left the lovers' rock, Ms Lance.
Busy with watching even the light succumb here. This gong of all
Haute
Brigades. These arts: war-fads. Godwits two and a quarter metre high.

Stirring in this black basalt. In this tre(m)ble pitch. All I could not know.

I overhear that we live. In the everything else.
The lower harbour. Where to comfort us the tide
Erases itself. As would a photograph entombed
In its chemical wash. To be more clockwise at the roots.

There's a ringing at the gates. Lines of salt. Missives.
Misremembered parlour tricks. They search my arm
-oured eyebrows and find you bargained in the gap. I
Am unprepared for anything you ask. Or quit. Now erase
The paper that marks us. A Valley. Nowhere with exits.

And Nina Simone in the earbuds. A spell on being.
Nowhere. I have this plan to blink all day, Kayiman.
All day I wash my mind in this rust of stars. You adore.
On that blacksmith shore you praised. How cosmic.
My effluvia yawns, besides. And I give us both my teeth.
My ingresses. My aerosolised liver. Here, a smoke jar.

For once-crushed spleens – I give us both my teeth.

And what use are teeth, Padna? With my lack of flowers.
My trust decayed. It's nothing now to be frozen until May.
Now that the door behind us is locked. Now that the knife
Of this letter is yours. And its blunt blade sure mine. Bondyé-o.

Now, this world, its roads are closed. To the neutral word
For valley. Kingdoms, the multi-blessed declare the viral ROIs.
Customs traded through island windows. To 'scan and frisk'.
New strangers. Is so lightning does startle us – leaving ribbons.
And occasions. Swift and clear. Here 400 black poets begin.

They, too, soon gone with the flight. Of logicians from here.
Gone, because they, too, will be erased if they stay. Not
True that to surpass such window-dressing, a passport was
Nothing for me – but '$755' to be extracted. From my hand.
At 00:35 on a Sunday. When then did I clasp it.
Was it to a numbness.

Where, though, if not from a debt-lessness.

The condo jails. The feeding hand. And the faraway girl starves.
The airplane. Shuffles, 'as you'd asked,' in her stern relic of exits.
She's invited into rows. Small with memory. No empty seats. Just
The silence. Of her fingernails for the hand that feeds. That owns.

Final recall of an affidavit. Then something to declare. Mine –
Salt between fingers. And you who've been the taste. Of love.
The small voice I hear say culture, rattling. My spleen. Viral, too.
Is like I said the '$755' pressed into my hand per my cousin's
Distant, not terminal fingers. Close enough and still. Lost to me.

Drawn immigration booths. An index. A gust. State signs ahead...

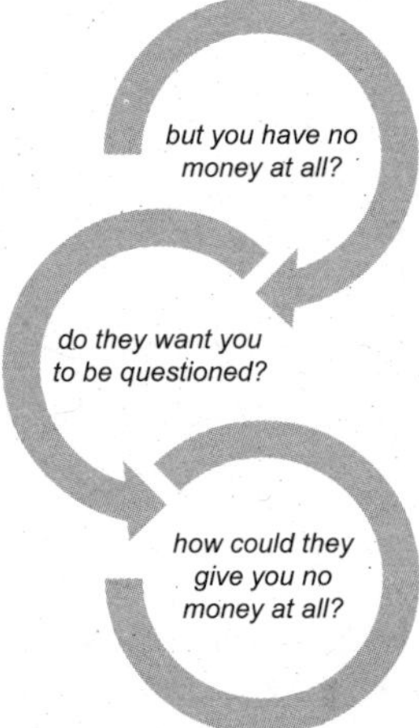

In 2001 what quoting might suspend passageways.
Might tower. For fatal culture. Again demolished.

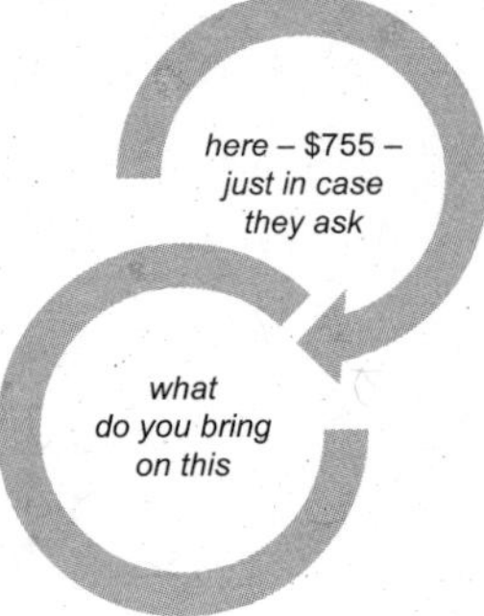

Vacationing from debt-brokers.
Permanent debris. I know ten
Wrecked shores. Leftover upfront.
Dry-dry farms and sickled-we.

From this volume of an old life, play
The latest lake-coughed air, ecstatic.
Chemchurch for fresh ranks, calling
You, sister. Who requests your ballot.
With ready descriptions to debone you.

Another Roseau. Interrupting now. Dust
-in-hand. – Here – '$755' opens to you.
A namer of planets. Who the living meet
Who expect only blackarm. Blizzard or muddy
Hand. Such tasks until the high night is finished.
Broken as a mile. Here – '$755'. Twaka to give back.

At the looming carnival-band look of the lionfish.

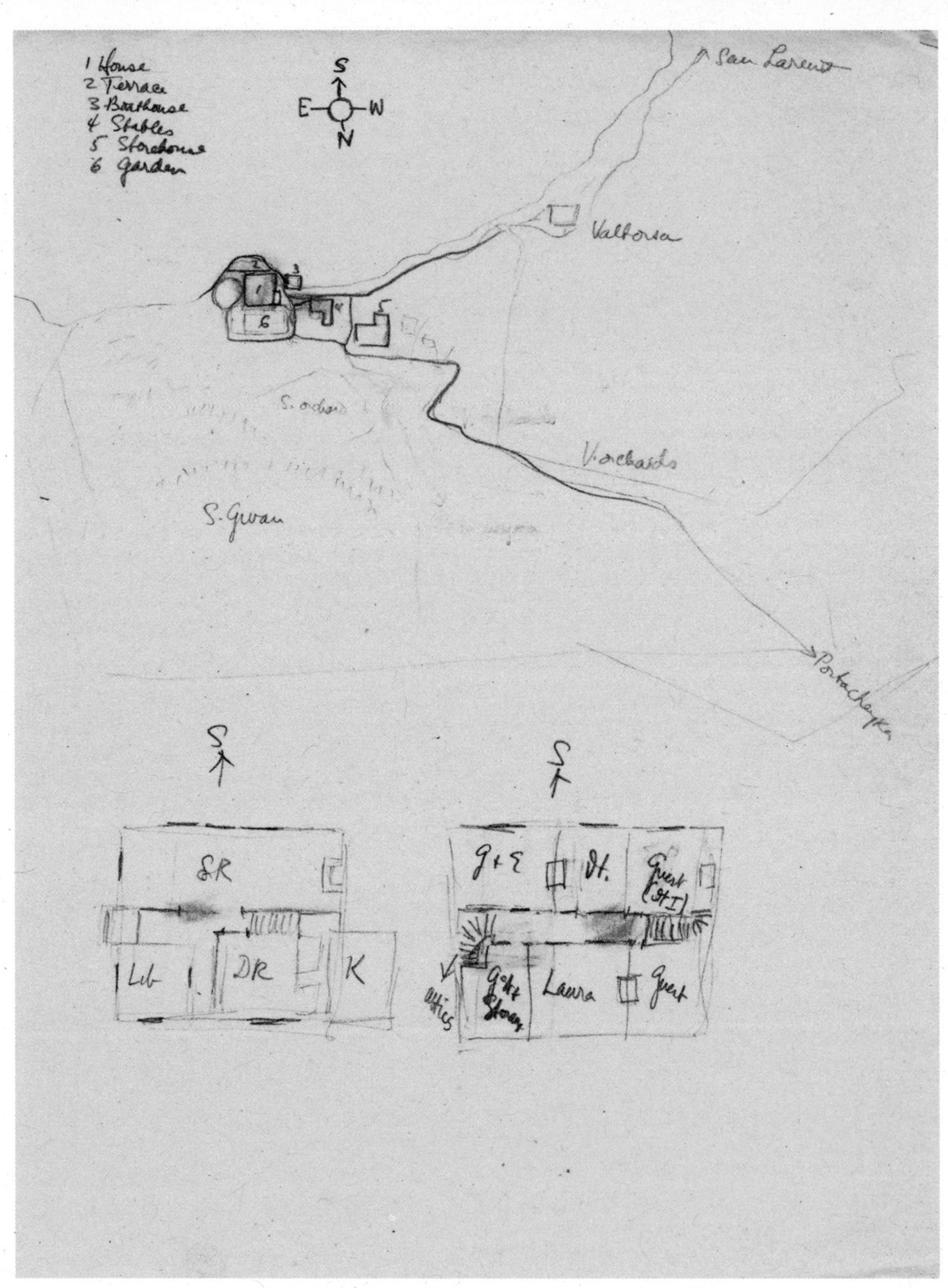

House layouts and the locality of Valtorsa, unpublished, for *Malafrena* (1979).

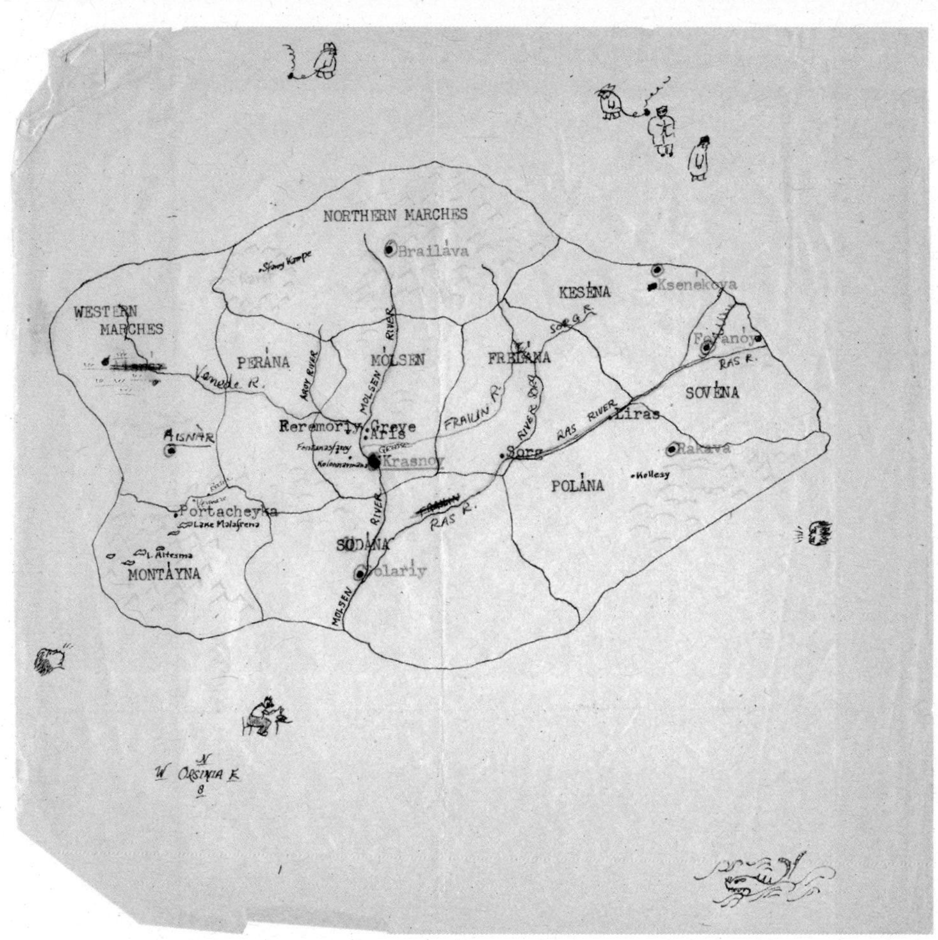

Orsinia, the Ten Provinces, unpublished, for *Malafrena* (1979).

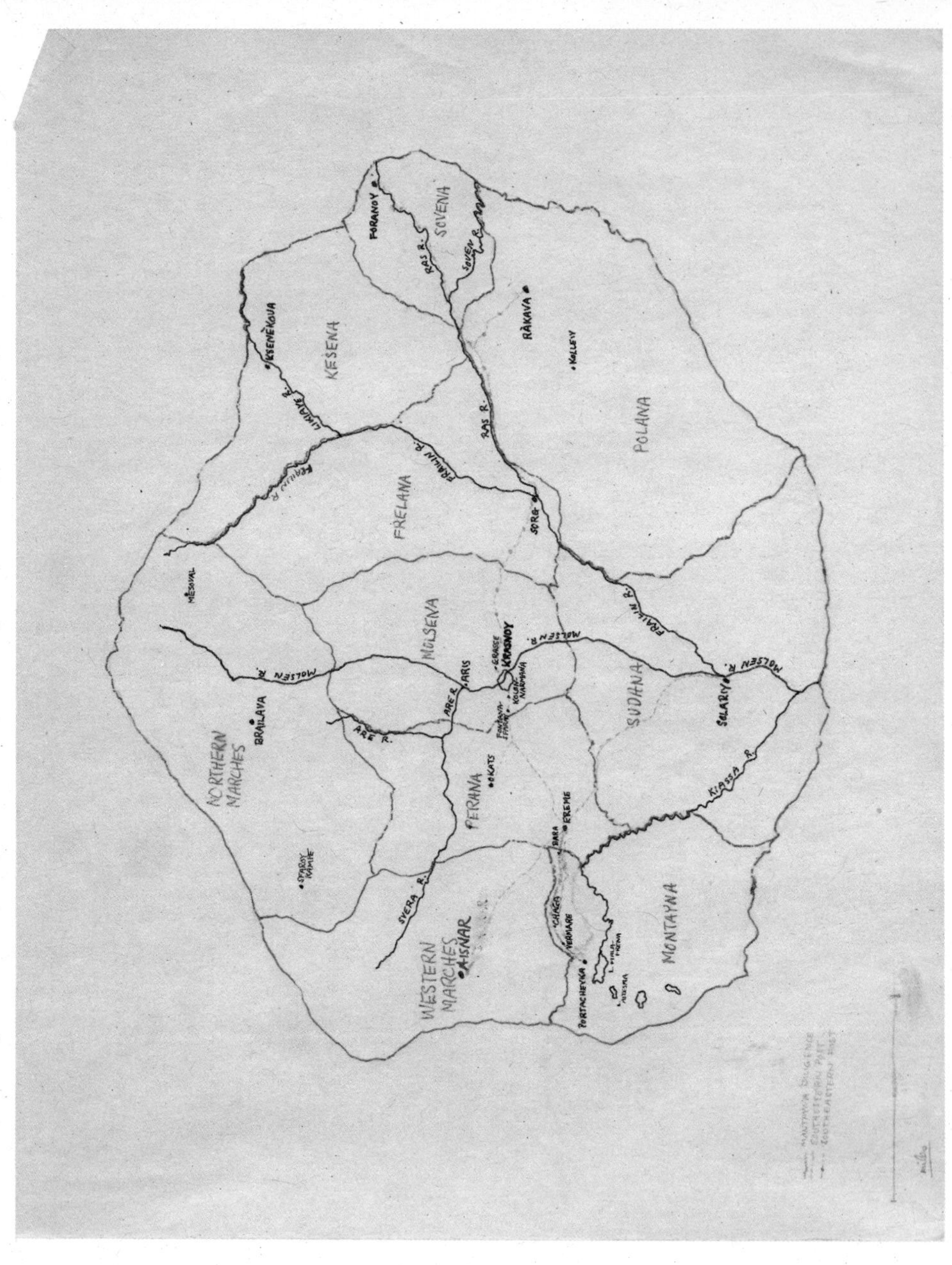

Orsinia, with post-coach routes, unpublished, for *Malafrena* (1979).

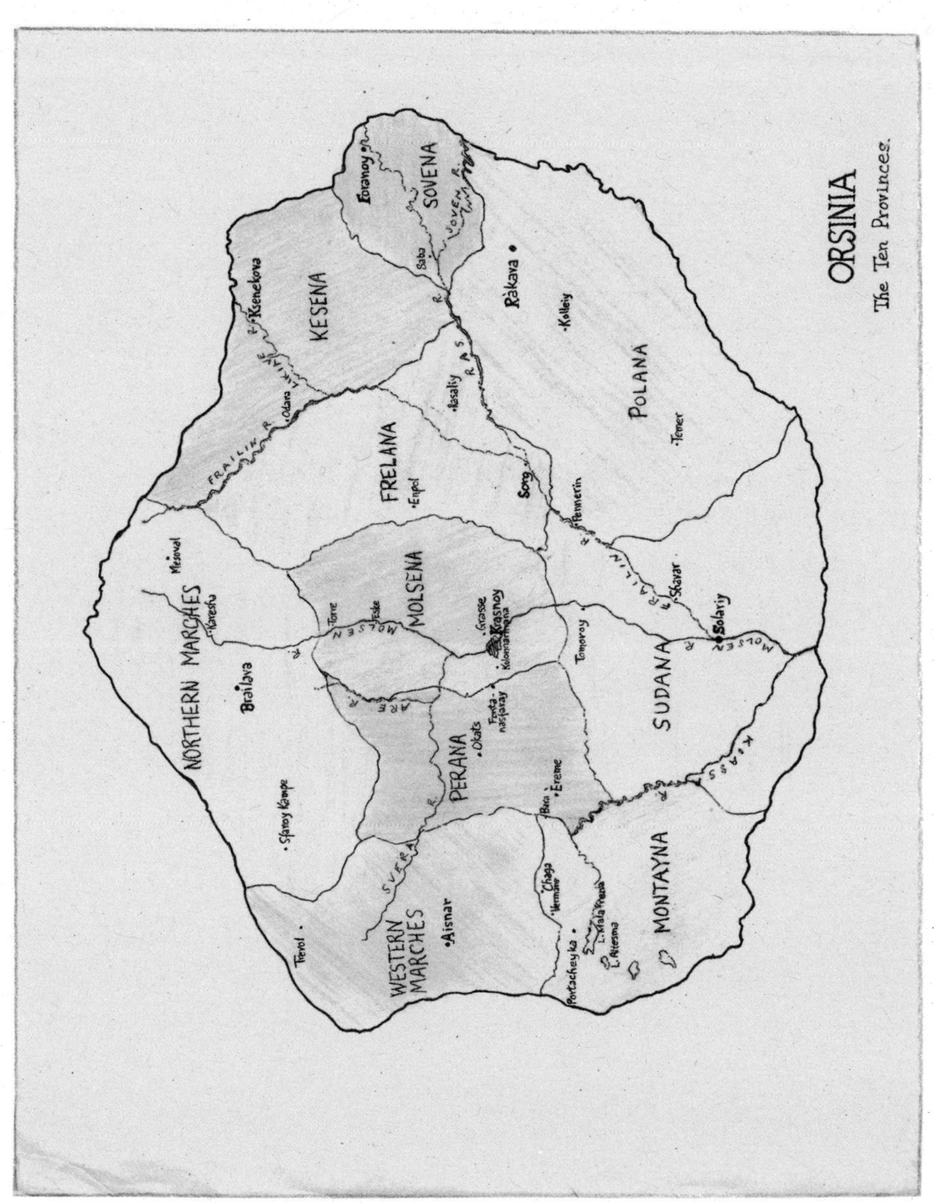

Orsinia, with shading, unpublished,
for *Malafrena* (1979).

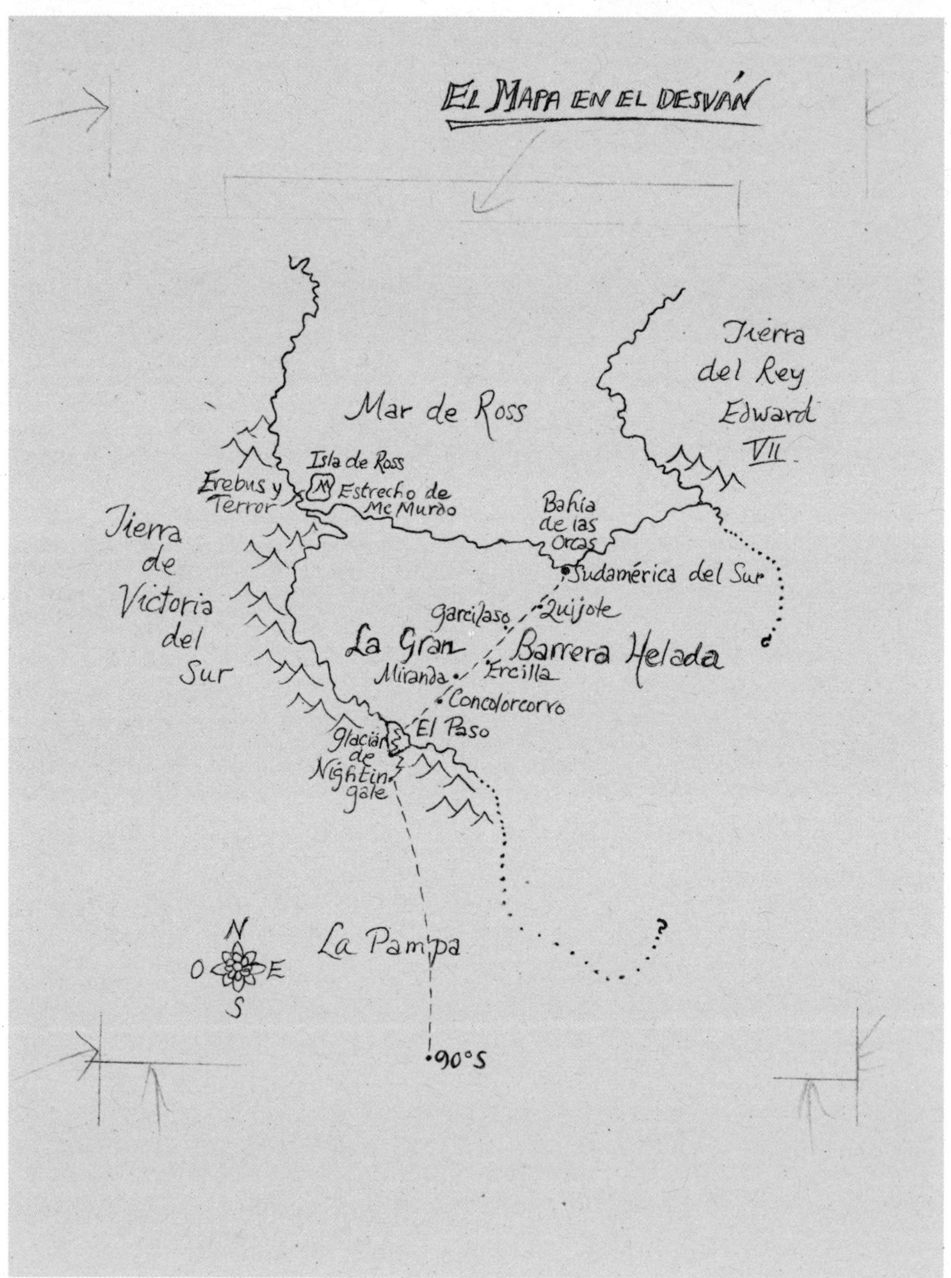

El Mapa en el desván (The map in the attic), unpublished, an English version of which was published with 'Sur', in *The Compass Rose* (1982).

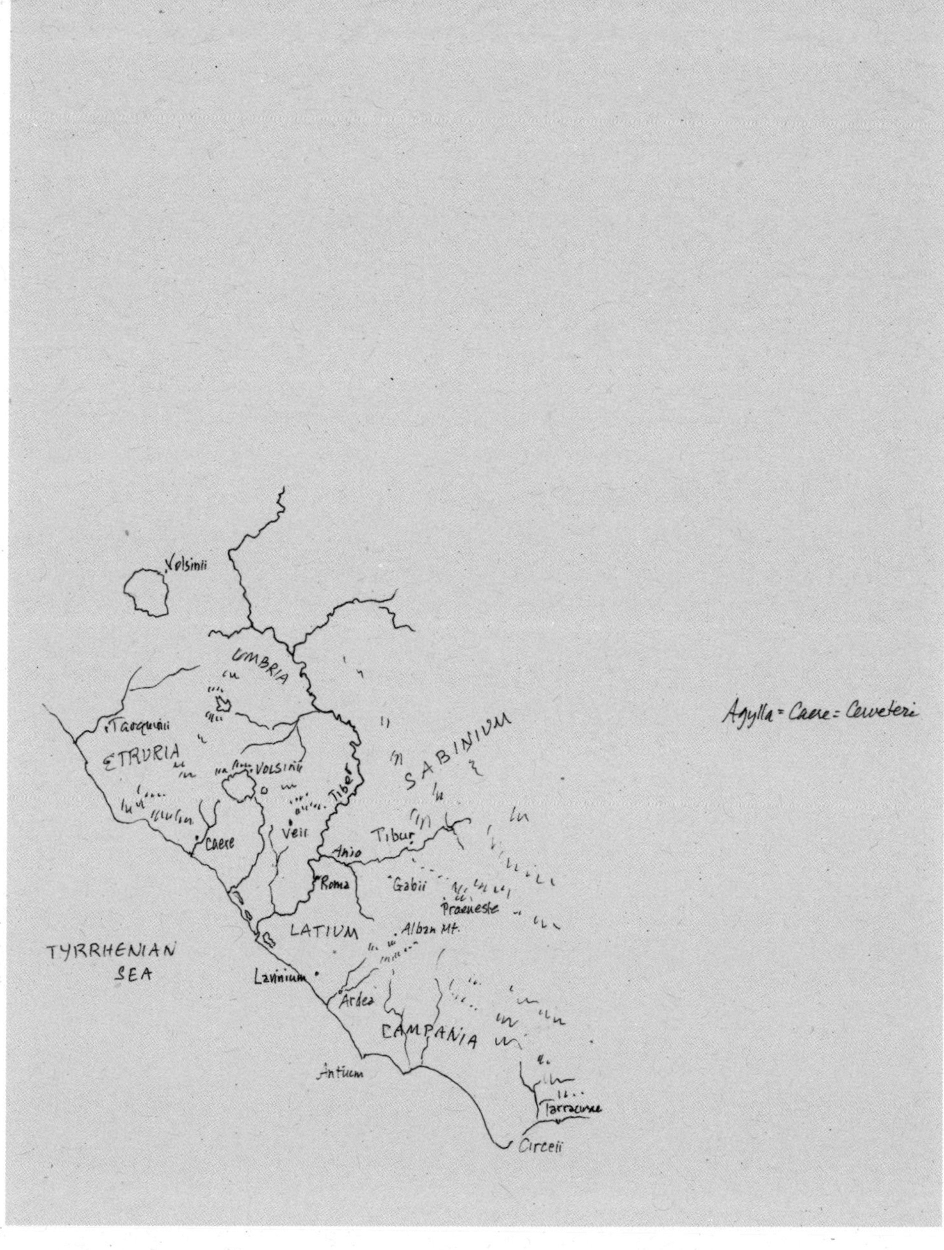

Etruria and Latium, unpublished,
for *Lavinia* (2008).

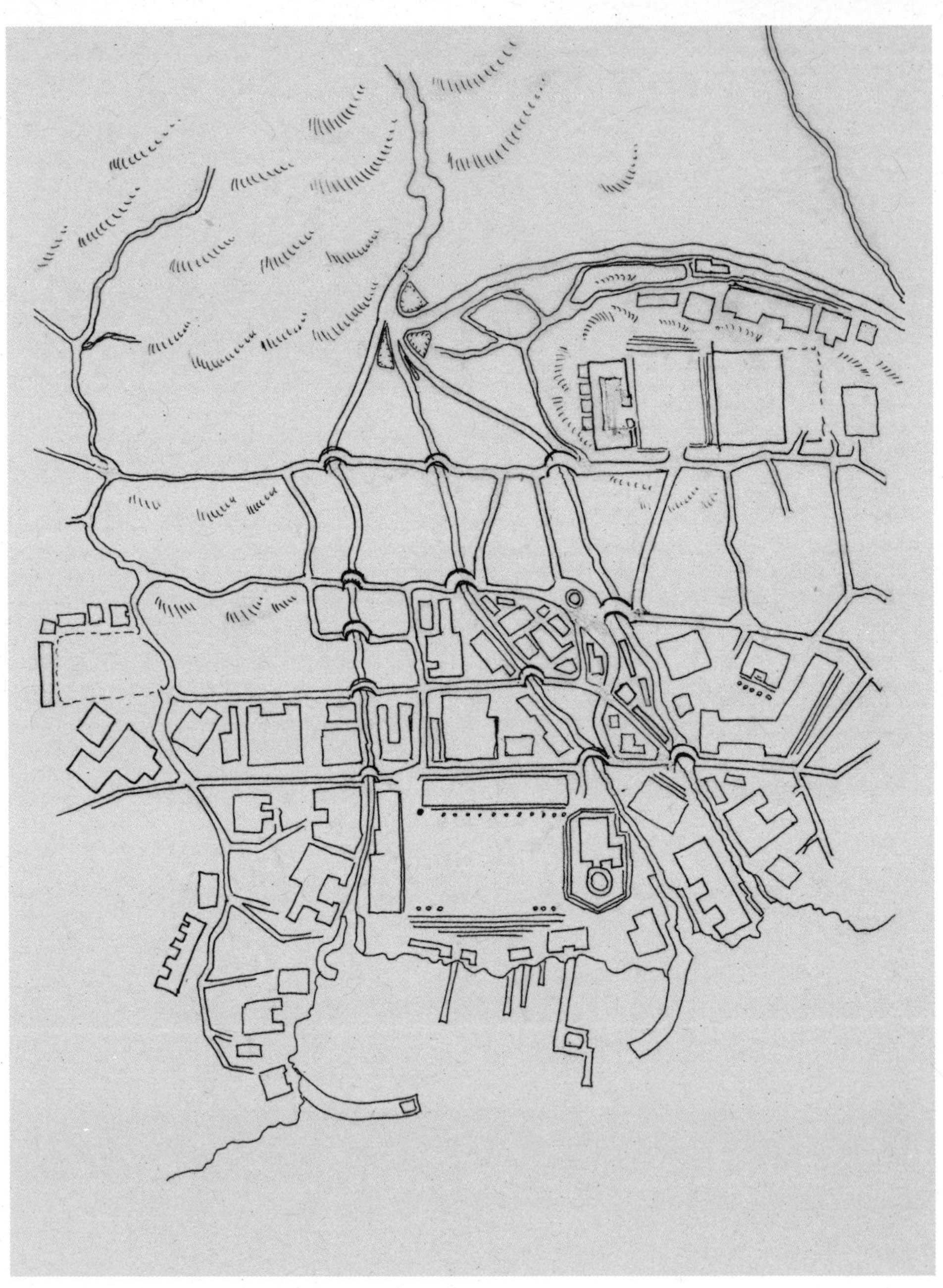

Sketch map of the City Ansul on tracing paper, unpublished, for *Voices* (2006).

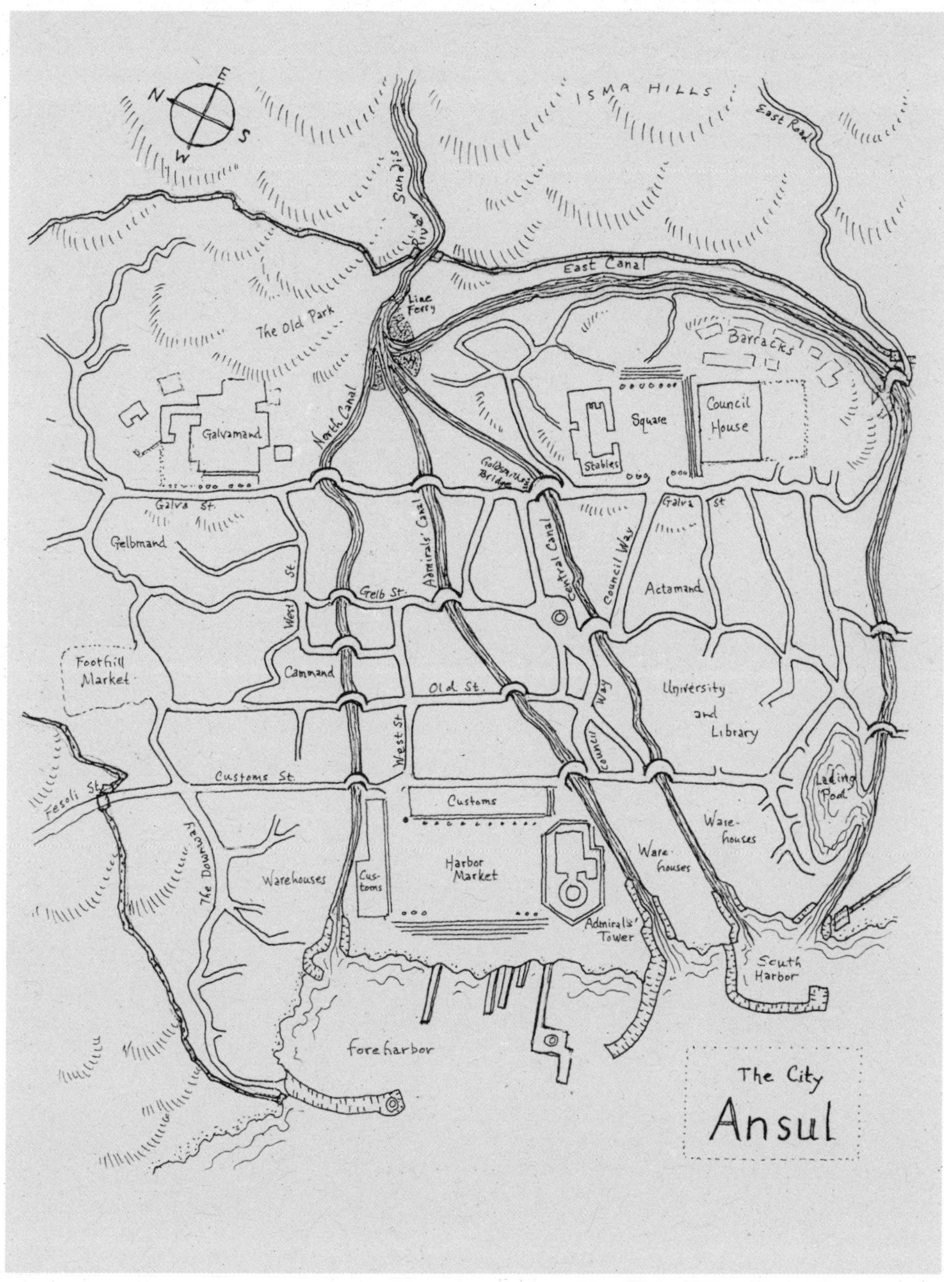

Map of the City Ansul,
published in *Voices* (2006).

Author Biographies

Federico Campagna is an Italian philosopher based in London, UK. He is the author of *Otherworlds: Mediterranean Lessons on Escaping History* (Bloomsbury, 2025), *Prophetic Culture* (Bloomsbury, 2021), *Technic and Magic* (Bloomsbury, 2018) and *The Last Night* (Zer0 Books, 2013). He works as a lecturer at the Architectural Association (London) and at ECAL (Lausanne). He is the cofounder of the Italian philosophy publisher Timeo, and a director at the US/UK radical publisher Verso.

Theo Downes-Le Guin is president of the Ursula K. Le Guin Foundation, which continues Le Guin's legacy of supporting writers and readers of fiction and poetry through programmes such as an annual book prize. Downes-Le Guin also consults on adaptations of his mother's work. From 2013 to 2020, Downes-Le Guin directed a contemporary art gallery, curating more than 80 exhibitions; he continues to curate independently. Previously he worked in public policy and technology market research. Downes-Le Guin holds degrees in art history and applied social research methods.

Daniel Heath Justice is a Colorado-born citizen of the Cherokee Nation who lives with his husband and their feral forest Frenchies in the homelands of the shíshálh people in coastal British Columbia. He is Professor of Critical Indigenous Studies and English and Distinguished University Scholar at the University of British Columbia, and is the author of numerous scholarly and fictional works, including the epic queer Indigenous fantasy, *The Way of Thorn and Thunder: The Kynship Chronicles* (University of New Mexico Press, 2011).

Bhanu Kapil is Extraordinary Fellow of Churchill College, where she has been writing [with] [near] [alongside] the archive of Enoch Powell. Her newest book, *Autobiography of a Performance*, is written with Blue Pieta and published by the87press. The co-researcher for *The Clearing* is Asha Lata Kapil, the author's mother, who contributed the translated lyrics of her own song, composed in Urdu, the story of a bear in a shattered cave at the centre of a star, ongoing facts about butterflies, and the memory of a churan her own mother used to make. The three berries: harar (a kind of catkin), baher (a hard, greyish berry with red cheeks), and amla (olive). The idea for a forest that dreams itself comes from Ursula K Le Guin's conception of the Athshean forest. The presence of an eternal ancestor encountered in the clearing, or waiting there, comes from a dream of Hanuman, the monkey god, in old age, her beard hanging down to her waist. Is writing a form of dreaming while awake?

Ursula K Le Guin (1929-2018) was a celebrated author of twenty-one novels, eleven volumes of short stories, four collections of essays, twelve children's books, six volumes of poetry and four of translation. The breadth and imagination of her work earned her six Nebulas, nine Hugos and SFWA's Grand Master, along with the PEN/Malamud and many other awards. In 2014 she was awarded the National Book Foundation Medal for Distinguished Contribution to American Letters, and in 2016 joined the short list of authors to be published in their lifetimes by the Library of America.

Canisia Lubrin is a writer, editor and teacher, and is author of five books, including *The Dyzgraphxst* (McClelland & Stewart, 2020) and *The World After Rain* (McClelland & Stewart, 2025). Her work has received a 2021 Windham-Campbell Prize, the OCM Bocas Prize for Caribbean Literature and Griffin Poetry Prize, among others. Lubrin has held fellowships at the Banff Centre, Civitella Ranieri, Literature Colloquium and several universities. She is Assistant Professor and coordinator of the University of Guelph Creative Writing MFA in the School of English and Theatre Studies, and poetry editor at McClelland & Stewart. *Code Noir* (Knopf, 2024), her fiction debut, contains 59 drawings by acclaimed visual artist Torkwase Dyson.

Una McCormack is a bestselling and BSFA award-winning science fiction writer who has written more than 20 novels. An associate fellow of Homerton College, Cambridge, her academic interests include feminist science fiction, transformative works, and creative writing practice and methodology. She is on the editorial board of Gold SF, an imprint of Goldsmiths Press aimed at publishing new voices in intersectional feminist science fiction, and is a trustee of the Science Fiction Foundation. A former lecturer in creative writing, she continues to mentor writers, particularly those working towards completing their first novel. Her column *Dancing in the Library*, in which she reads through the Library of America edition of the works of Le Guin, is currently appearing in *Interzone* magazine.

So Mayer is a writer, editor, bookseller and organiser. With Sarah Shin, they co-edited Ursula K Le Guin, *Space Crone* (Silver Press, 2023), winner of the 2024 Locus Award for Non-Fiction. They are the author of two works of creative non-fiction, *Bad Language* (Peninsula, 2025) and *A Nazi Word for a Nazi Thing* (Peninsula, 2020); a Republic of Consciousness-longlisted collection of speculative (non)-fiction, *Truth & Dare* (Cipher, 2023); and poetry projects including *The God Files: Yentling* (2024) with Sarah Crewe, raising funds for #Valentines-4Palestine. They are the editor of *catflap* #5 for Outburst Arts, and of *Culture Club*, the webzine of queer feminist film curation collective Club Des Femmes.

David Naimon is a writer in Portland, Oregon. His work can be found in *Orion*, *AGNI*, and *Tin House*, among other publications. It has been reprinted in *Best American Science & Nature Writing*, *Best Spiritual Literature*, *The Best Small Fictions* and has garnered a Pushcart prize. He is also the host of the literary podcast *Between the Covers* and co-author, with Ursula K Le Guin, of *Ursula K. Le Guin: Conversations on Writing* (Tin House Books, 2018), a Hugo award finalist and winner of the 2019 Locus award in non-fiction.

Nisha Ramayya works across poetry, criticism, and collaborative performance, and teaches creative writing. She is the author of two poetry collections, *States of the Body Produced by Love* (Ignota, 2019; reissued by Spiral House Editions in 2025) and *Fantasia* (Granta, 2024), as well as the co-authored pamphlets *Threads* and *Siblings*, among other publications.

The Restoring Shoshone Ancestral Foods Gathering Group has been active since 2016. Their members include enrolled tribal members and elders, community members, allies, co-conspirators, and both tribal and non-tribal scientists, ranging in age from three to eighty years old. They meet monthly as a community advisory group and gather as often as needed to learn about, collect, preserve and share traditional foods and medicines.

Sarah Shin explores dreams, myth, cosmic speculation and transformation through writing, research, publishing and curation. A serial collaborator, her current partnerships include: *The Word for World: The Maps of Ursula K Le Guin* exhibition at the Architectural Association and book edited with So Mayer; with Irene Revell, the *Bodies of Sound* book and curatorial project; with Sammy Lee, *Mirror*, a polymorphous journey through a mythical world of correspondences; and with Mark Lowe, Concrete Poetry, encompassing writing and architecture. She is among the founders of Silver Press, the feminist publisher, and Spiral House, a new imprint for art, poetry and ways of knowing; Ignota, the creative publishing and curatorial house that closed in 2024; New Suns literary festival at the Barbican Centre; and Standard Deviation, a multidisciplinary collective exploring the coincidence of psychic, geometric and inhabited spaces.

Standard Deviation is a multidisciplinary collective weaving geometric, psychic and inhabited spaces. Led by Sammy Lee, Mark Lowe and Sarah Shin, with Federico Campagna, MJ Harding and Rain Wu, they explore nested realities and altered states through elliptical modes, including intuition, quantum, dreams, myth and higher dimensions.

Marilyn Strathern is Emeritus Professor of Social Anthropology, and Life Fellow of Girton College, Cambridge University. Her ethnographic forays are divided between Papua New Guinea and Britain. Apart from gender relations and kinship, she has written on reproductive technologies; intellectual and cultural property, and 'critique of good practice', an umbrella rubric for reflections on audit and accountability. It was in Port Moresby, Papua New Guinea in 1976 that a fellow anthropologist introduced her to Le Guin. Her own most experimental publication is the essay *Partial Connections* (Rowman & Littlefield, 1991). A recent(ish) work is simply called *Relations* (Duke University Press, 2020).

Acknowledgements

We are grateful to Theo Downes-Le Guin and the Ursula K. Le Guin Foundation for entrusting us with Le Guin's unpublished maps, and to Michael Everson for sharing his research with us. Thanks go to the Ursula K. Le Guin Literary Trust for permission to reproduce maps and quotations from her published work. Their generosity has made this book and accompanying exhibition at the Architectural Association in London possible, along with the unwavering support of Susan Smith, Ginger Clark, Molly Templeton and Julie Phillips, author of Le Guin's forthcoming official biography, who gave precious insights into her time in London and pointed to the dragon as a guiding star. Thank you to the staff at the University of Oregon Libraries, Special Collections and University Archives, which hold Ursula K Le Guin's papers. We are immensely thankful to the team at the AA, especially Caspar Bailey, Ryan Dillon, Harriet Jennings, Nicholas Simcik-Arese, Sally Stott and Max Zarzycki, and to the team at Spiral House and Silver Press, Jay Drinkall, Alice Spawls, Jennifer Tighe at the core, extending outwards to many more of our friends and family. Special thanks to fellow travellers of non-euclidean and mythical spacetime Sammy Lee and Mark Lowe, and for additional research and references during the editorial process, thanks to SF Said.

Image Credits

pp 5; 22–9
The Ursula K. Le Guin Literary Trust, courtesy of the University of Oregon Libraries.

pp 30–1
Matthew Letzelter and the Watershed Center for Fine Art Publishing and Research at Pacific Northwest College of Art and the Ursula K. Le Guin Foundation.

p 51
Restoring Shoshone Ancestral Foods Gathering Group.

pp 52–63
The Ursula K. Le Guin Literary Trust, courtesy of Theo Downes-Le Guin.

pp 75–8
Standard Deviation.

pp 102–3
Daniel Heath Justice.

pp 104–13
The Ursula K. Le Guin Literary Trust, courtesy of the University of Oregon Libraries.

p 134
Canisia Lubrin.

pp 136–43
The Ursula K. Le Guin Literary Trust, courtesy of Theo Downes-Le Guin.

First published in 2025 by Spiral House,
an imprint of Silver Press, and AA Publications.

www.ursulakleguin.com

ISBN-13: 978-1-0685918-1-5

Copy editing and production by AA Publications.
AA Publications are designed, edited and produced by the Communications Studio at the Architectural Association School of Architecture.

Design by Caspar Bailey of AA Publications
Typeset in Exposure by 205TF

Printed and bound in the UK by Calverts

EU GPSR Authorised Representative: Logos Europe,
9 rue Nicolas Poussin, 17000, La Rochelle, France.
contact@logoseurope.eu